C000194479

TIME PLEA

A LOOK BACK AT BIRMINGHAM'S PUBS

Based on the Mitchells & Butlers archive

ANDREW MAXAM
with David R. Hassall

FOREWORD BY CARL CHINN

Front Cover:
CROWN, 36/37 Broad Street / King Edward's Place, 1901 (W). Established in 1781. The home of William Butler's Crown Brewery, before he moved to Cape Hill with Henry Mitchell. Much altered and extended over the years. In the 1990s it was renamed **Edwards** and today stands at the heart of Birmingham's thriving Broad Street and Brindley Place pub scene.

Back Cover:
(Top left) **GOTHIC**, 1 Great Hampton Street / Great Hampton Row, Hockley. For further details see page 66. (Top right) **GATE INN**, 183 Icknield Street / Camden Street, Hockley, 1952. Complete with its distinctive turret that was later removed. See page 70. (Lower right) **KING EDWARD V11**, 275-279 Corporation Street / Staniforth Street, 1999. Dating from 1905 and designed by Wood and Kendrick it is seen here when trading as **Monkey Mick's Cider House** though for many years this pub was called the **Ben Jonson.** Pub now closed. (Lower left) **OBSERVATORY**, 44A Barker Street / Hunter's Road, Lozells, 1924. For further details see page 86.

Dedication: To all those who have worked at the Cape Hill site together with managers and staff at Birmingham's pubs over the past 130 years.

In memory of

Michael Richard Maxam (1932-1983)

John Albert Simonds (1929-2002)

Leo James Griffiths (1903-1977)

ISBN: 0 9543913 0 6

First published 2002 by Crown Cards, Smethwick, West Midlands.
Email: info@maxamcards.co.uk   Website: www.maxamcards.co.uk

Designed, typeset, printed and bound by Adlard Print & Reprographics Ltd, Ruddington, Nottingham.

CONTENTS

FOREWORD

Professor Carl Chinn, MBE, Ph.D.

Landscape. When we bring that word to mind we tend to draw upon images of painters such as Turner, Gainsborough and Birmingham's own David Cox and to see before us mountains and hills, cliffs and rocks, fields and hedgerows, rivers and streams, hay wains and harvests, animals and birds. For so many of us, to talk about landscape inevitably means focusing solely upon the rural so that it is inconceivable to link landscape with the urban environment.

Poets and writers of all kinds have contributed to the praising of the countryside and to its glamorisation as an idyllic place. In so doing they have counterpoised towns and cities as dark, dreary and depressing locations that cannot be regarded as having a landscape.

But the urban space is a landscape in its own right and in particular the urban industrial landscape has its features and attractions. Birmingham stands as a forthright example of this contention. The great gas holders of Nechells and Saltley vie for attention with factories such as Longbridge and HP Sauce; whilst churches like Saint Martin's and Saint Chad's call out as landmarks as much as do the Central Mosque and the Sikh Gurdwara on the Soho Road. Roads and canals cut through the city, dividing it and bringing it together, whilst parks and riverside walks allow the rural to live still in the city.

Such grand features are surrounded by the smaller yet as important elements of the urban landscape – the houses, schools and shops. But Birmingham's urban landscape is dynamic and ever changing and we are in danger of losing one its most important elements – its pubs, especially its back-street pubs. Generations of Brummies grew up to learn to give directions by referring to the location of well-known pubs such as 'The Gate' at Saltley. And generations of Brummies grew up knowing as a matter of fact that in the older working-class neighbourhoods, pubs were crucial lynch pins in the community and in themselves were vital in fostering neighbourliness and community spirit.

Pubs were more than a place to drink. They were social, sporting and neighbourhood centres. Usually boasting a bar, a smoke room and an outdoor where older married women would sit and drink, these pubs were spots to escape from the rigours of life and to come to so as to celebrate national and municipal events as much as those that impinged only upon local families. And local they were. Drawing their regulars from a small area, back-street pubs were embedded within their neighbourhoods and just as the local folk depended upon the pubs for a major facility so too did the pub depend upon the people of the neighbourhood.

But with the redevelopment of Birmingham and the clearance of the older localities, many pubs were swept from history. More recently, others have fallen victim to the decline of Birmingham breweries and the desire by many pub chains to focus upon high street locations and to abandon the back street local.

Tellingly, not only back-street pubs are disappearing at an alarming rate but so too are the large, inter-war pubs that were built in the council estates developed in those years. Go to the Warstock and Yardley Wood to see this unfortunate trend. The Warstock, the Dog and Partridge, the Haven and the Bagnell have all gone and have entered the memory as much as have the Star in Aston, the Gladstone Arms in Sparkbrook, and the Phoenix in Park Street.

Within a generation a key piece of Englishness will be gone and young people will not know the meaning of having a local. But at least they will be able to see that which has been lost. There are too few photographs of the back street pubs of Birmingham setting them in their neighbourhoods and there are too few of those in the districts that emerged in the 1920s and 1930s. 'Time Please' has been called on them, but because of this book 'Time Please' they will not be lost from history. The authors have brought them back to life with the photographs they have saved and for which they feel they are trustees for the rest of us. They are to be congratulated on bringing to view a major part of our history.

INTRODUCTION

This book brings together part of a collection comprising over 380 photographs of pubs and off-licences from all over Birmingham, many never previously published, taken from the early 1900s up to the late 1960s. Most of these came from an archive of 1,000 photographs formerly housed at the Cape Hill offices of Mitchells & Butlers, but now in the ownership of the authors. In this volume, we will deal with pubs from the M & B stable, which also includes Atkinson's Brewery Ltd of Aston and William Butler & Co Ltd of Wolverhampton. It is hoped that a volume two will include the Black Country.

The Story of Mitchells & Butlers

The closure at the end of 2002 of the Cape Hill Brewery where brewing has taken place for over 120 years, marks the end of an era for brewing in Birmingham. Although Cape Hill lies just beyond its boundary in Smethwick, this still leaves Birmingham without a major brewery. Mitchells & Butlers, founded in 1898, rose to become the region's largest brewer, taking over many smaller companies on the way until itself becoming the subject of subsequent takeovers. It is to be hoped that the name itself will not disappear into the midst of time.

Henry Mitchell (1837-1914) started brewing at the Crown Inn, Oldbury Road, Smethwick, a homebrew pub owned by his father. He soon took over from his father and started supplying other pubs with his increasingly popular beers including light mild ale, becoming a common brewer. Soon he outgrew his existing premises and in 1878 he acquired a 14-acre site at Cape Hill. In that year, the first Artesian Well was sunk and work started to construct a new brewery. The first brew took place in July 1879. Henry Mitchell's was incorporated as a private company in 1888 and two years later had 86 tied houses, some of which are featured in this book.

Meanwhile his future partner William Butler (1843-1907) first became licensee of the London Works Tavern, London Street, Smethwick. Quickly gaining a reputation as a home brewer of note, he moved to larger premises in 1876 at the Crown, Broad Street, Birmingham where he had previously worked as a barman. He, too, sold his beer to other Birmingham pubs and in order to keep up with demand soon built an impressive tower brewery at the back of the Crown. At one time this plant was producing 5,00 barrels a week. This building survived until the 1980s when demolished to make way for the International Convention Centre. Butler's Crown Brewery was incorporated in 1895, by which time he too was a common brewer to a chain of tied houses.

Both Henry Mitchell and William Butler provided loans to local publicans, thus tying them to their product and ensuring that they had guaranteed outlets for their beers. The interest charged on these loans could then be used towards further expansion, which in the 1890s was very much the name of the game. Birmingham was changing rapidly, swallowing up neighbouring villages. Increasing innovations in transport, especially with the railways meant that breweries from other parts of the country such as Burton-on Trent started to view other towns as potential areas of expansion. Local brewers were forced to respond by developing their own pub estates, though large capital sums were required. Arthur Guinness had initiated the rush for generating capital by becoming the first brewery of several to float on the stock exchange in 1886. The capital raised was used to buy the freehold or long-term leases on existing pubs. The rush for property led to a dramatic increase in prices, fuelling a tied-house war. An economical way of buying pubs was to acquire the brewery that operated it. Birmingham's emerging big players started buying out the struggling smaller brewers who could not compete; a classic case of economies of scale. So, in 1898 both Mitchell and Butler joined forces, transferring all their brewing operations to Cape Hill. It was a case of growing big to survive, something they did at a spectacular rate. Within two years the Cape Hill site increased to 60 acres; by 1914 up to 93 acres by which time a no. 2 brewery was opened with a capacity of 30,000 barrels per week.

Takeovers and Mergers

This list illustrates the rapid growth of M & B through takeovers until 1967 and subsequent major changes thereafter on a national basis, until closure of Cape Hill: -

1898	Henry Mitchell Co joins with William Butler's Crown Brewery; formation of Mitchells & Butlers at Cape Hill site
1899	Vulcan Brewery, Alfred Homer Ltd, Aston
1900	James Evans' Brewery, Perry Barr
1913	Cheshire's Windmill Brewery, Windmill Lane, Smethwick
1919	John Charles Holder's Midland Brewery, Nova Scotia Street, Birmingham
1920	J. Jordan & Co, Oldbury
1932	T Russell Ltd, Wolverhampton
1939	Highgate Walsall Brewery Co. Ltd, Walsall
1950	Thatcher's Bristol Brewery Ltd, Newport, Monmouthshire
1951	Darby's Brewery Ltd, Greets Green, West Bromwich
1959	Atkinson's Brewery Ltd, (Aston Park Brewery) Queen's Road, Aston, Birmingham
1960	William Butler & Co Ltd, Springfield Brewery, Wolverhampton (who had also bought out in 1955 Aston Model Brewery of Frederick Smith, Lichfield Street, Birmingham. This may explain how M & B were so strong in Aston, despite being a stronghold of their main rivals, Ansells.
1961	Bass, Ratcliffe & Gretton, Burton-on-Trent (merger)
1967	Bass Charrington United Breweries (south west & north east England), this was the truly national merger; the company became Bass, Mitchells & Butlers
1989	Government legislation introduced to limit number of tied pubs. Many pubs sold. Bass move into acquisition of hotels e.g. Holiday Inns.
1990s	Many pubs sold off either individually or to other groups. National branding of retained pubs commences e.g. O'Neill's (1994) Harvester (1995)

1999   Bass joined with Punch Taverns to acquire many pubs of Allied Domecq's estate
2000   Bass sells brewing business to the Belgian brewer, Interbrew. Brewing and pubs business now separated.
2001   Government blocks Interbrew's takeover of Bass brewing. Bass changes name to Six Continents plc. Further sales of pubs deemed unsuitable for future rebranding. American brewer Adolph Coors Co emerges as the surprise buyer of Carling brand and 4 breweries including Cape Hill.
2002   21 March: Coors announce end of production at Cape Hill brewery, to be closed in December of that year.

The Story of Birmingham's Pubs

The evolution and development of Birmingham's pubs over the past 150 years has roughly echoed that of the common brewers. The early Victorian period saw the emergence of privately managed homebrew rather than brewery-owned beerhouses. Many of which, architecturally, blended into their surroundings that were usually adaptations of older houses or cottages. The quality of the ale these beerhouses produced was variable and over a period of time the tied house system whereby the common brewers supplied the ale became more prevalent. The 1869 Wine and Beerhouse Act was able to restrict the number of licensed premises by restoring the power of the local magistrates. More legislation followed with the purpose of reducing levels of drunkenness. The common brewers became richer, and with the market becoming more competitive as already explained under the History of M & B, many homebrew pubs struggled to survive and gave way to the common brewers.

The late Victorian period from the 1880s into the 1900s saw the widespread rebuilding of many city and suburban pubs. The expertise of Birmingham's architects was called upon to build striking, distinctive buildings such as the **Barton's Arms**, Aston and the sadly lost **Woodman**, Easy Row. These architects included the prolific James & Lister Lea; William Jenkins, Henry Naden, also Wood & Kendrick of West Bromwich. The buildings they produced were generous in their use of terracotta and attention to detail on the outside, not to mention superb quality glazed tiling, carved woodwork, mirrors, stained and engraved glass, wallpaper, brass bar fittings, etc.

The turn of the century saw the introduction of the Birmingham Scheme (also known as fewer and better), an agreement made between the City Council and the local breweries such as M & B. This voluntary scheme encouraged the brewers to surrender the licences of the obsolete and inadequate public and beerhouses mainly in the inner city areas on the understanding that they would open a smaller number of bigger, "reformed" improved houses mainly on main roads in the suburbs. For an early example, see the **Red Lion** at King's Heath. The idea was that out in the suburbs, a larger house could draw people in over a wider area, with less competition - more profitable for the brewers and creating a reduction in casual drinking which is what the Council wanted. Between 1904 and 1914, one thousand licenses disappeared in Birmingham.

In the 1920s and 30s this larger house prevailed - refer to the **Antelope**, Sparkhill, **Stockland Inn**, Erdington and **Yew Tree Inn** at Yardley as a few good examples. These were pubs M & B were proud of; with well laid-out formal gardens, car parks, bowling greens and assembly rooms where food was provided with comfortable tables and seating. Women were encouraged as well as men. Architects who came to prominence in this period included the firms of Holland W. Hobbiss and Bateman & Bateman.

Many pubs suffered bomb damage during World War 2, and in the 1950s and 1960s slum clearances and rebuilding in both central and inner city areas decimated the numbers of old pubs and beerhouses, some of which never should have gone but were swept away as was apt for the time. The building of the Inner and Middle Ring Roads as well as motorways and general road widening in the 1960s also reduced the number of pubs. Areas such as Aston, Nechells, Newtown and Ladywood were particularly affected, though the outlying areas such as Erdington, Handsworth, Hall Green and Harborne fared somewhat better. During this time, as new estates developed at places such as Shard End, Castle Vale and Perry Beeches, an austere plain looking replacement type of pub was being built.

Relative calm was restored in the 1970s and 80s although the emergence of Wine Bars was seen as competition. Occasional demolition of pubs was often due to road widening schemes. However during the 1990s and early 2000s, traditional pubs have continued to decline, as the concentration of themed bars, clubs and restaurants has risen, particularly in the Brindley Place and Broad Street areas. Together with the rebuilding of the new Bull Ring and the Mailbox and Star City developments, this is to be broadly welcomed as progress as Birmingham moves ever forward. However we should not let all of the fine old buildings that have served so well over the last century or more disappear forever.

It has been a fascinating and enlightening experience for the author to undertake the research for this book (I tried to go round as many surviving pubs as possible, as well as checking out what was there in place of the non-survivors). With the information assembled regarding opening / closing dates; architects' details and change of trading names plus any other information gleaned, this book should appeal to those who, over the years have spent time socialising, working and living their life in Birmingham's fine old pubs and at the same time to keep them informed of their destiny.

Key to the captions

The captions to the photographs show the name of the pub at the time of the photograph was taken; its address (including the neighbouring street when located on a corner); followed by the date of the photograph (precise or estimated); followed by a (W) which refers to the pub being listed in White's Street Directory of 1869; followed by known details of architects where known; opening and / or closure dates as contained in records from the archive. However, records are missing, so for the sake of completion, the author has tried to fill in the gaps with some dates from a variety of other sources; these are marked with an asterisk (*). It can only be assumed that the information from the M & B archive is accurate, but any inaccuracies that do occur in a work of this nature are obviously to be regretted. Every effort has been made to provide the correct information, and any improvement as regards dates, etc. will be welcomed for use in a revised edition.

BIRMINGHAM CENTRAL AREA (postcodes B1-5)

KING EDWARD V1, 17 Parade / Newhall Hill c. 1925 (W). A good old-fashioned pub dating from c. 1835, bought by M & B in 1922. Survived until 1996* when it was demolished and replaced by a car showroom.

RED LION, 53 Church Street/ Cornwall Street, 1903. A former hotel, the current building replaced an earlier inn. In the mid nineteenth century, it was the meeting place of the British Association for the Advancement of Science. Renamed the **Old Royal** in the early 1960s and still going strong today.

WESTWARD HO, 232-5 Broad Street / Granville Street, c. 1963. Opened 22 November 1924 as the **Granville Inn**, the architect was Arthur Edwards. Renamed **Westward Ho** from 14 October 1963. Later reverted to the Granville, the pub is now called **O'Neill's** and is at the heart of the many bars and clubs that now occupy Broad Street.

COLMORE, 16 & 18 Church Street / Barwick Street c. 1968. The prominent sign reads Entrance to Mirabelle Lounge (Ground Floor) & Barbara's Lounge (First Floor) in Barwick Street. Renamed the **Gaiety** on 14 November 1969, then became the **Cathedral Tavern**, 1990*. Its licence was surrendered 24 March 1999*.

WHITE HORSE HOTEL, 30 Congreve Street / Great Charles Street, 1929 (W). The West Bromwich architects Wood and Kendrick rebuilt this majestic pub and restaurant in 1906 at a cost of £17,484 for the buildings only. Its function rooms were used by many including the Rocket Club, a gathering of Birmingham Bohemians. The clubroom could easily seat 140 persons. Closed 30 June 1965 in order to make way for the proposed new library.

CHAPEL TAVERN, 123 Great Charles Street / Ludgate Hill c. 1965 (W). Listed in Pigot's Directory in 1828. By 1897, it was part of William Butler's Crown Brewery empire. Note the police phone box on the corner and the newly built Post Office tower in the background. Pub closed on 8 May 1966, a compulsory purchase order made by the Council for the Inner Ring Road. The staircase of a pedestrian footbridge over Great Charles Street Queensway now occupies this site.

WHITE SWAN INN, 119 Edmund Street, 6 September 1960, seen here when still an Atkinson's house. After refurbishment by M & B in the early 1960s, the room on the left became the Cob room and on the right, the Cygnet lounge. The pub was leased to Berni Inns in 1968. Its licence was surrendered 24 March 1999* and eventually converted into offices.

WHITE HART INN, 19 Paradise Street c. 1950 (W). When J. Roussel Ltd moved out of no. 20 in 1951, the shop was incorporated into the White Hart as the wine and spirit merchant "Aux Amis des Bons Vins". The M & B Birmingham City order office was also here for a while. The pub closed on 15 August 1965 due to the Inner Ring Road scheme, and the Fletchers Walk complex now occupies the site. Its licence was transferred to the **Hole in the Wall**, Dale End that opened for trading 30 September 1966.

SHAKESPEARE TAVERN, 4 Lower Temple Street c. 1950. A beer and wine house that gained its full licence in 1915. The pub still survives but alas the ornate gas lamp has long gone! Records state that the M & B Ales sign was removed in May 1952.

TEMPLE BAR, Lower Temple Street c. 1963. Stood next door to the Shakespeare. Formerly an Atkinson's pub that was transferred to M & B on 15 February 1963. Closed in 2001* and converted to a retail outlet.

MIDLAND TAVERN, 235 Lawley Street (now Middleway), 19 April 1962 (W). Formerly a Henry Mitchell pub. Dating from 1900 this terracotta pub was an early rebuild by West Bromwich architects Wood and Kendrick. Surprisingly, it had a beer only licence until 1954. Pub closed for demolition, April 1982.

VICTORIA, 48 John Bright Street / Station Street, 16 June 1950. In the late 1870s, this part of Birmingham had a reputation as a slum area, a problem that vexed the nearby Council. Their response was to create John Bright Street, cut in 1881 at a cost of £31,000 and was named after the industrialist who had been a city M.P for over 30 years. The street connected the civic centre via Hill Street down to the Horsefair en route to affluent suburbs such as Edgbaston. In 1883 a Thomas Heatley was manager of the Queen pub in the old thoroughfare called New Inkleys (renamed Station Street, 1884). In 1884 he became licensee of the Queen Victoria , John Bright Street and by 1894 the pub was one of William Butler's chain with beer supplied from the Crown Brewery at Broad Street. The Alexandra Theatre seen next door was rebuilt in 1936, after having opened in 1901 as the Lyceum. By 1904, the pub was known simply as the Victoria, as is still the case today.

OLD CONTEMPTIBLES, 176 Edmund Street / Livery Street, 1 May 2002. Formerly known as the **Albion** until its name changed to the Old Contemptible, 31 January 1953. Its nickname is the O.Cs.

QUEEN'S HEAD (old building), 28 Steelhouse Lane c. 1920 (W). This old building was eventually replaced by the rather plain one still here today. Over the road at no. 134 the **George and Dragon**, another James & Lister Lea pub, is fondly remembered: a pub rebuilt in 1926 and closed in 1960.

SHAKESPEARE INN, 31 Summer Row / Lionel Street, c. 1920. A traditional pub still relatively unspoilt at the time of writing. The students from the nearby College of Food often frequent the pub, as the author knows from his own experience! Another M & B pub, the **White Swan** stood at no. 61 Summer Row until closure in 1933 on a site later occupied by Willies Wine Bar. Now part of the refurbished Summer Row and Hotel complex.

ST. PAUL'S TAVERN, 24 Ludgate Hill c. 1962 (W). An old beerhouse that gained its full licence in 1918. Had the feel of a traditional "back street boozer" until refurbished and extended in the late 1980s. Today there is the **Mongolian Bar** (a stir-fry restaurant) and Xanadu (now Chameleon) bar next door where the old pub was.

CABIN, Priory Queensway, (off Corporation Street), 1966. Seen here when newly built, it opened on 26 October 1966 and was renamed the **Priory** in 1994*. Atkinson's had owned a Cabin pub and restaurant nearby at 50 & 52 Union Passage, which had closed in 1966.

ROEBUCK, 152 & 154 Hurst Street / Skinner Lane, 14 May 1965 (W). Formerly a home-brew pub. Some neighbouring houses were merged into the pub over the years. Now called the **Village Inn** and little changed externally since this picture was taken.

BRUNSWICK, 52 Lancaster Street / Lench Street c. 1964 (W: George & Dragon). Closed for trading 14 January 1967* and now disappeared within the Lancaster Circus Queensway.

GUNMAKERS' ARMS, 92 Bath Street / Little Shadwell Street c. 1964 (W). The name of the pub reflected the predominant industry in this area. A former Atkinson's pub that still thrives today.

DUKE OF YORK, 13 Duke Street, Gosta Green, 1962 (W). A long-standing local closed in the summer of 1974 and later on, the city's last gas lamp was removed from this street in January 1975. The whole street was to disappear due to expansion of the Aston University site.

WHITE TOWER, 126 Lawley Street (now Middleway) / Vauxhall Road c. 1932 (W). This building replaced an earlier inn and dates from 1932. Some of the surrounding houses owned by M & B were "demolished by enemy action" during the war. Note the sign on the lamppost advising "Caution Recreation Ground", referring to nearby Lawford Street. Still open as a Banks's pub known as **Moriarty's**.

THERE'S AN

Quite near to you

M&B

HOUSE

No. 4 The "WOODMAN," Easy Row Birmingham

THE "WOODMAN", which was rebuilt in 1891, at one time played an important part in the civic life of Birmingham.

In the days before Joseph Chamberlain entered the Town Council it was the custom for many of the leading Aldermen and Councillors to meet nightly in the smokeroom and discuss the business of the town. Besides themselves, a number of prominent and influential inhabitants used to meet there and they freely criticised the actions of the Council, actual and proposed.

To listen to the talk at the "Woodman" was to feel the pulse of the town. Of course, in those days of a hundred years ago and more, the taverns occupied a very different place in the social life from the public houses of to-day. Nearly all the shopkeepers and manufacturers lived on the premises and only the wealthiest of them resided in the suburbs. In the winter evenings they would meet together in some smokeroom like the "Woodman," where every man had his own chair and his own tankard.

The "Woodman" was the last of the old taverns. The earliest landlord of the house dates back to 1820, but there is little or nothing to be learned of the "Woodman" until it was bought, about 1850, by James Onions, from the "Eagle and Ball" in Colmore Street. This old tavern had long been the rendezvous of actors from the Theatre Royal. Most of the customers followed Jem Onions to the "Woodman" and it became the recognised theatrical house of Birmingham. Their portraits, steel engravings, wood cuts, adorned the walls of the smoke-rooms. The walls were hung with old playbills recording the famous visits of Italian Opera. This collection was dispersed long ago.

The "Woodman" appears to have been a house for carriers' vans, and in its early days the Shrewsbury coach used to make its last call before leaving Birmingham.

The present building of the "Woodman" was intended to recall the old traditions. Its smokeroom has the old-fashioned ingle-nook fireplaces, with oak beams elaborately carved and decorated. On the tiled walls of other parts of the house are many pictures of old Birmingham.

The woodman, axe in hand, whose figure is the modern sign, was executed in stone by a well-known sculptor of 57 years ago, A. E. Naylor.

And so long as the life of Joseph Chamberlain is written, so long will the name of the "Woodman" survive.

For everybody who tells his civic career is bound to add a sentence, usually in ignorance of the social conditions of the period, that before his time, the business of the town was settled over a pint of ale at the "Woodman".

The Lord Mayor of Birmingham, Alderman J. C. Burman, makes a presentation of an Electric Clock to Mr. W. A. Baines, Works Manager of Messrs. Burman Cooper & Co. Ltd. upon his retirement, at the "Woodman", Easy Row, Birmingham.

Photograph by kind permission of Birmingham Gazette Ltd.

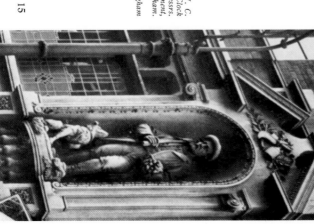

WOODMAN, 5 Easy Row, (Deerstalker Magazine, April 1949), (W). Rebuilt in 1892 by architect Henry Naden, it had been used as a meeting place for the Council. This truly magnificent pub closed on the last day of 1964 and the whole of Easy Row was demolished to make way for the uninspiring Paradise Circus complex.

left **TROCADERO**, 18 Temple Street, 1969. This is a Grade 2 listed building, dating from the mid 19th century by the architect Charles Edge, originally for Norwich Union Fire Office. The attractive yellow glazed front was added later, with an Art Nouveau flavour. A former Atkinson's pub, still open.

below **CROWN INN**, Hill Street & 65 Station Street, 1902. A former Butler's Crown Brewery hotel. The records state that in 1943 Birmingham Corporation rented the next door basement, no. 25 Hill Street for use as an air raid shelter. Pub still trading.

STAR VAULTS, 114 Dale End, 1966 (W). Formerly called the **Star Vine Vaults**. Closed 6 July 1966 for the redevelopment of Dale End and the Priory Square Shopping Centre. Its licence was transferred to the newly opened **Cabin**, Priory Queensway.

CASTLE INN, 5 Prospect Row / Brueton Street, c. 1946 (W: un-named beerhouse). Closed in 1965* due to redevelopment of this area. Now Prospect Row and Brueton Street have been swallowed up by the Jennens Road dual carriageway.

DIGBETH, DERITEND & BULL RING AREA

BROOK VAULTS, 51 Jamaica Row, c. 1962. Dating from 1886 by architects James & Lister Lea in Flemish style, it was originally known as the **Criterion**. *The Caterer and Hotel Proprietors' Gazette* said of this pub it was *"a building second to none for beauty of design and elaborate decoration"* and reported that takings had trebled since its rebuild. A former Atkinson's pub which closed in 1974* but now demolished to make way for the Wholesale Market.

NEW INN HOTEL, 191-194 Bromsgrove Street, 27 August 1953 (W). A rebuild from 1884 also by James & Lister Lea. This fine looking building was bought by M & B in 1934 but closed in 1972* for demolition and the site is now part of the Wholesale Market.

BIRMINGHAM ARMS, 1 Moat Row / Sherlock Street East, 1 September 1957 (W). Another rebuild from 1886 again by architects James & Lister Lea, replacing an earlier inn. The Smithfield Vegetable Market can just be seen (far right). Closed for demolition in 1973*, this area also now forms part of the Wholesale Market.

BIRMINGHAM HORSE, 21 Moseley Street / Barford Street, Deritend, c. 1962 (W). A former Atkinson's beerhouse which closed 20 December 1970* and this part of Moseley Street has also been lost to the Wholesale Market.

BRUSHMAKERS ARMS, 5 Cheapside, 25 May 1965 (W). A Butler's beerhouse. This pub stood opposite the old Wholesale Meat Market. Closed in 1972*, now demolished and swallowed up by the new Wholesale Market.

FOUNTAIN INN, 93 Cheapside & 46½ Alcester Street, c. 1929 (W), with the licensee Charles Albert Hands standing proudly in the doorway. This Atkinson's house was mentioned in Pigot's Directory, 1828. Still open for trading.

right
The Royal George old building

below
The Royal George new building

ROYAL GEORGE, 143 Digbeth / Park Street, 31 January 1957 (W: as **London Museum and Music Hall**). It's nickname was the "Mucker" - allegedly so called due to the mucky state of the customers who were mainly barrow boys from the Bull Ring, although the name is also a Brummie slang word for friend or mate. M & B also owned the little florist's shop at no. 142. The old pub closed 3 January 1962 and the current building complete with the splendid ship sign built on the same site opened for trading 8 July 1964*.

PHOENIX, 3 Park Street, 1965 (W). Dating from the early nineteenth century, the Old Phoenix Inn offered "livery and stabling". A former Atkinson's pub, seen here after closure (5 August 1965*) when up for sale, prior to eventual demolition.

OLD BULL'S HEAD, 80-81 Digbeth, 1940 (W). Mentioned in Sketchley's Directory of 1767. Handy for the tram, right outside! Now renamed the **Kerryman.**

MATADOR, 205 East Court, Bull Ring Centre, 1 March 1965. The appropriately named pub opened on 20 December 1963 within the new Bull Ring, to the left of the "Witzy Doo" restaurant. It received a licence from the **Crown**, 50 Snow Hill. Later renamed **Blarney Stone** (1995*), it closed in 2000*. Now demolished as the 21st century Bull Ring development takes place.

WANDERING MINSTREL, 1st Floor, West Mall, 311 Bull Ring Centre, 1 March 1965. The pub opened on 27 May 1964 receiving a licence from the **Corner**, 133/4 Moor Street. Renamed **49ers** in 1989*. In the 1990s it traded under a procession of names: **M & Ms**, **Peacocks**, **Genesis** and **Emma's Bar**. Its licence was revoked on 8 June 2000*. Now demolished as the 21st century Bull Ring development takes place.

ACOCK'S GREEN & TYSELEY

Foxholes Hotel, Acocks Green   PN1656

FOX HOLLIES, Olton Boulevard East / Fox Hollies Road, c. 1952 as seen on a postcard. The pub opened on 21 September 1928, receiving its licence from the **St. Vincent Arms**, 259 St. Vincent Street, Ladywood which had closed a day earlier. The architects were Wood & Kendrick. Closed in 1997* to make way for a supermarket.

A close-up view of the fox stone relief above the front porch of the **Fox Hollies**. This plaque has now been incorporated in the *Lidl* supermarket that now stands on the site of the pub.

RED LION, 1145 Warwick Road, c. 1946. This old building was demolished in September 1982* and a new pub built.

DOLPHIN, 1203 Warwick Road / Dolphin Lane, 1930. The pub opened on 16 May 1930 replacing an old coaching inn but was demolished in 1992*. The former Lord Mayor of Birmingham, Councillor Freda Cocks was a licensee here. Now the site is occupied by an *Aldi* supermarket.

GOSPEL OAK, Gospel Lane / Gospel Farm Road, c. 1948. Built on the site of Gospel farm on the boundary with Hall Green, the pub opened on 18 November 1932; the architects were James & Lister Lea. Still open today trading as the **Red Rooster**.

BRITANNIA INN, 909/911 Warwick Road, Tyseley, 1 April 1961. This former Holder's inn was demolished in 1973* and replaced by the current larger building.

ASTON

1902. BARTONS ARMS ASTON.

BARTON'S ARMS, 144 High Street / Potters Lane, on a postcard dated 1914 (W). One of Birmingham's most famous pubs, still in tact. Dating from 1901 and designed by Mr. Brassington of James & Lister Lea although it replaced a previous building that had been on the site since 1840. It boasts a superb display of tiling and tile paintings by Minton; together with fine stained glass and a snob-screen. Joe Davis played snooker here; over the road at the Aston Hippodrome stars such as Charlie Chaplin and Laurel and Hardy performed. Threatened with demolition in the late 1960s it underwent a thorough restoration in 1980 and still survives today.

NEW PEACOCK, 49 Aston Road, c. 1919 (W). The pub closed for trading 10 April 1957* and its licence was transferred to the **Grotto Inn**, 250 Camden Street, Brookfields. The site is approximately where the Aston Expressway starts just before Dartmouth Circus.

DUKE OF YORK, 213 Aston Road / Pritchett Street, 13 July 1961 (W). Over the road from the New Peacock was the Duke of York, which suffered a similar fate after it closed on 21 September 1972*.

BRITANNIA INN, 287 Lichfield Road, opposite Aston Station, 1 September 1957. A former Henry Mitchell's pub that was rebuilt in 1898-1900: the architects were Wood & Kendrick. This pub, complete with Britannia's distinctive figure looking down Lichfield Road, survived the threat of closure in the 1970s and is still open for thirsty commuters on the Cross City Line!

HEN & CHICKENS, 129 Rocky Lane / William Henry Street, c. 1965 (W). This beerhouse, rebuilt in 1900 is by architects Wood & Kendrick and still survives; now called **Shanahan's - The Food House**. An extension on the side of this pub gives it a spacious outlook.

WHITE HORSE, 187 Victoria Road, c. 1950 (W). M & B bought this pub back in 1913 but closed it in 1971* to be replaced by housing.

ALMA TAVERN, 123 Alma Street, Aston New Town, c. 1946 (W). This pub stood on the west side of Alma Street between Clifford Street and Gerrard Street but was closed in 1968*. All this area has been completely rebuilt.

STAR INN, 88a Aston Road North / Yates Street, c. 1965 (W). A former Atkinson's pub which closed at the end of 1972*. Now the site of a police depot alongside the Aston Expressway.

SALUTATION INN, 30 Alma Street, Aston New Town, 26 May 1965. A former Butler's of Wolverhampton house. Exchange Buildings can be seen on the right. The pub closed in 1968* and this part of Alma Street leading to Six Ways has now been redeveloped.

MAZEPPA, 39 & 41 Yates Street / Thomas Street, c. 1930 (W). A beerhouse that gained its full licence in 1951. Probably took its name from the Polish nobleman and Cossack soldier Ivan Stepanovich Mazeppa whose amorous adventures inspired Lord Byron to write a poem about him in 1819. Pub closed in 1969* as this whole area was cleared to make way for the Aston Expressway.

ROYAL GEORGE, 28 Park Road / Tower Road, Aston Cross, 23 February 1961 (W). Did the locals at the Royal George appreciate the pungent odour from the nearby H.P Sauce factory? Formerly a beer and wine house, it was granted a full licence in 1961. By 1976 demolition of the surrounding shops had started and the pub closed on 6 June* of that year. The pub has now gone and the land has been taken over by the factory.

AVENUE HOTEL, 253 Park Road / Queen's Road, 25 May 1965 (W). A former Butler's of Wolverhampton house. By 1969* the pub and this part of Park Road had gone forever - under the Aston Expressway. Note the bus stop in Queen's Road which reads: *"This side reserved for buses on the occasions of first class matches on Saturdays at Villa Park"*.

TOWER ARMS, 31 Potters Hill / Tower Road, 25 May 1965 (W). Another Butler's of Wolverhampton house. By 1972* the pub had gone and Potters Hill no longer exists.

RED LION, 228-230 Lichfield Road & 2 Vyse Street, c.1965 (W). Osborne Tower is under construction, far right. The pub's licence was surrendered on 9 January 1977*, falling victim to road widening. Vyse Street has been truncated.

RESERVOIR INN, 469 Lichfield Road / Cuckoo Road, c. 1924 (W). Pub still survives not far from Birmingham's infamous Spaghetti Junction.

KING EDWARD VII, Lichfield Road / Aston Hall Road, 29 March 1961. Dating from 1904, the architects were Wood & Kendrick. The pub is still open but has been under threat of closure.

VICTORIA PARK INN, 221 Victoria Road / Upper Sutton Street, c. 1960 (W). This former Atkinson's pub like its neighbour the **White Horse** closed in 1971* for replacement housing.

QUEEN'S HOTEL, 165 Church Lane / Queen's Road, 23 August 1960 at 2.45pm, according to the clock! A former Atkinson's pub whose signs are still promoting their bitter and brown ale. Time was up for this old pub as well as its licence was surrendered on 18 September 1969* to be transferred to the **Adventurers** in nearby Queen's Road (opened 2 October 1969).

UPPER GROUNDS HOTEL, Trinity Road / Bevington Road, c. 1964. A former Butler's of Wolverhampton pub, still satisfying the needs of thirsty Aston Villa supporters!

BALSALL HEATH

EARL GREY, 76 Pershore Road / Balsall Heath Road, c. 1969. The architects Wood & Kendrick were used to carry out alterations back in the early 1920s. The pub closed in 1998* although the building still stands, converted into housing.

CROWN INN, 63 Wenman Street / Mount Terrace, 25 April 1962. This old beerhouse was to close 31 March 1967 due to redevelopment of the area.

BATH TAVERN, 111 Mary Street, 20 August 1959 (W). A former Holder's beerhouse that was granted a full licence in 1951. The shutters were down when this photo was taken as they were for good when it closed in 1973*. Housing now occupies this site.

EAGLE TAVERN, 189 & 191 Mary Street c. 1947. This beer-house was a new purchase for M & B back in 1939 and was granted a full licence in 1962. The pub's nickname is "Snackers". A faint *Wolverhampton Ales* painted brick advertisement can still be seen at the pub.

CASTLE & FALCON, 402 Moseley Road, c. 1960. This former Atkinson's pub is still open today. Now known as the **Ceol Castle**.

NEW INNS, 527 Moseley Road / Edward Road, 8 May 1967 (W: un-named beer house). Rebuilt in the 1890s. The sign was advertising the "Las Vegas Discotheque." Back in 1967, the DJ could have been playing such tunes as "*Puppet on a String*" or "*Hi-Ho Silver Lining*." Still open today.

LYTTLETON ARMS, 173 Balsall Heath Road, c. 1946 with a boarded-up shop next door. A beerhouse that was granted a full licence in 1962. Pub closed 13 April 1969* and this area has been completely rebuilt.

GLADSTONE ARMS, 178 Clifton Road / White Street, 8 May 1967 (W). This former Holder's beerhouse gained a full licence in 1951 but was to close thirty years later. Housing now occupies this site.

CLIFTON, 267/271 Ladypool Road / Clifton Road, 25 February 1965 (W). A beerhouse that was granted a full licence in 1955. This former Butler's of Wolverhampton pub is still open today.

BORDESLEY, BORDESLEY GREEN & LITTLE BROMWICH

RAINBOW, 160 High Street / Adderley Street, Bordesley, c. 1964 (W). This Atkinson's house was listed in a Birmingham Directory as early as 1767. Pub still open.

CLEMENTS ARMS, 30 Coventry Road / Upper Trinity Street, Bordesley, 22 November 1961 (Was called **Birmingham & Oxford Railway Inn** and later **Great Western Vaults** before its current name in the late 1870s). The first recorded licensee was William Pugh in 1835. He was also a cab driver. Multiple occupation licensees were common at the time. The lease was transferred to M & B in 1911 and the pub is still open.

DOLPHIN, 58 Coventry Road / New Bond Street, Bordesley, c. 1964. The pub's licence was surrendered on 14 January 1988* and is now demolished.

BULL'S HEAD, 173 Camp Hill, Bordesley, c . 1968 (W). This old inn was listed in Pigot's Directory in 1829 and closed for trading on 2 November 1975*. Now demolished.

LAMP, 133 & 134 High Street, Bordesley, c. 1964 (W). Another old inn listed in Pigot's Directory in 1828. A former Holder's house. Pub closed on 31 July 1974* and now demolished.

CORNER STORES outdoor, 106 Sandy Lane / Sampson Road North, Bordesley, c. 1945. The outdoor closed on 4 April 1957 due to redevelopment of the area. Sandy Lane has now become the busy Bordesley Middleway but the distinctive Holy Trinity Church on Camp Hill still stands.

GARRISON TAVERN, 110 Garrison Lane / Witton Street, Bordesley, 18 April 1961. The former Atkinson's house was renamed **Drover's Arms** before reverting to the **Garrison** and is now a Banks's pub. The cafe next door is now a newsagent.

SAMSON & LION, 42 Yardley Green Road / Blakeland Street, Bordesley Green c. 1948. A former Holder's beerhouse until this pub was rebuilt in 1922. The architects were James & Lister Lea. Pub still open complete with the distinctive clock, but the room in the roof has now gone.

CUSTARD HOUSE, Blake Lane / Blake Place, Little Bromwich, 25 February 1965. This unusually named pub took its name from a nearby farm. Gradually extended over the years, incorporating Alma Cottage to the east (1964) and property nos. 33/35 (1978). A former Atkinson's pub, still open today.

AVENUE, 470 Green Lane / Second Avenue, Bordesley Green, c. 1948. The pub by architect S. N. Cooke opened on 20 November 1931 and still thrives today having been renamed the **Potcheen Still**.

BROOKFIELDS & SPRING HILL

LAURELS, 92-96 Hingeston Street & 27-29 Prescott Street, c. 1960 (W). Closed 24 August 1970* and all trace of this former Atkinson's pub has now gone.

BROOKFIELDS TAVERN, 169 Hingeston Street / Pitsford Street, 18 April 1962 (W). This beerhouse had to wait until 1966 to get a full wine, beers and spirits licence. The pub has now gone, as has this part of Hingeston Street during redevelopment in 1970*.

CROWN STORES, Outdoor, 265 Camden Street / Ellen Street, c. 1928. Typical of many outdoors in the area that have long since gone. With the 2002 demolition of the nearby 1960s Brookfields Shopping Precinct, it will be interesting to know if the Brookfields name will survive.

Outdoor, 78 Springfield Street, 5 August 1964. Not long before the bulldozers moved in. Thomas Oliver Tyler was then the licensee.

SIR CHARLES NAPIER, 95 Rosebery Street / Camden Street, c. 1960. This former Atkinson's pub stood close to Rosebery Street Tram depot, which closed in 1968. The pub itself closed on 18 October 1970*. Now demolished.

COACH & HORSES, 93 Spring Hill, c. 1962 (W). One of Henry Mitchell's pubs. St. Peter's Church on George Street West can be seen (left), and Playfair's shoe shop is attracting a lot of interest (right). The recently renovated pub looks immaculate but was to close in 1970*. Alas, today all these buildings bar the church have now gone and a grassy bank is now prominent in this area.

WHITE SWAN, 10 Ingleby Street, 18 September 1961 (W). An old beerhouse that gained its full licence in 1958. The pub closed on 13 February 1966, the subject of a council compulsory purchase order. The whole of Ingleby Street, which ran from Spring Hill passage (off Spring Hill) to Monument Road (now Ladywood Middleway), has now gone.

BURTON STORES, 49 Parade, (between Edward Street and Clement Street), c. 1948. The pub closed on 7 June 1964, the subject of another Council compulsory purchase order for general redevelopment of this area.

CROWN INN, 14 Cope Street / Springfield Street, 12 April 1946 (W: as un-named beerhouse). Closed in 1965* and this area has been rebuilt with housing.

SUMMER HILL STORES, 32 & 34 Summer Hill Terrace / Powell Street, c. 1962. A former Holder's beerhouse that gained its full licence in 1950. Note the sign to drive slowly, as the Summer Hill Home for the Aged was next door. The pub closed in 1995* though the building is still standing with the windows boarded up. The Holder's crest is still visible on the exterior walls.

CASTLE VALE, CASTLE BROMWICH & SHARD END

SKYLARK, 106 Farnborough Road / Rhoose Croft, Castle Vale, seen here shortly after opening on 21 July 1966. Its licence came from the **Victoria Bars**, (formerly the **Olde Royal**), 17 Temple Row, which had closed two months earlier. Pub still open; now a Thwaites house. Less than forty years on, much of this area is again subject to redevelopment.

STAGECOACH, Newport Road, Castle Bromwich, c. 1966. The pub opened on 24 November 1966. Received a licence from the **Birmingham Arms**, 71 Hampton Street. On special offer in the window of the Good Cheer Cellars outdoor are bottles of Squires Gin 46/2 (£2.31); Martells Brandy 58/9 (£2.94); and Fine Douro Port 17/5 (87p). This pub was demolished c. 1998.

HUNTERS MOON, 220 Coleshill Road / Heath Way, Castle Bromwich. Shown here shortly after the pub opened on 29 March 1961 although a temporary premises had been open on the same site since 1952. Received a licence from the **Three Tuns**, 12 Smallbrook Street, a pub that had suffered from bomb damage during World War 2. Still open today though much altered from when new.

HEATHWAY, Heathland Avenue /Heath Way, Shard End, 17 April 1962, twelve days after it opened. Received a licence from the **Queen's Head**, 134 Hockley Street that had closed in 1956. Pub still open, little changed over the years although the outdoor has now been boarded over.

HARLEQUIN, Shard End Crescent / Heath Way, Shard End, c. 1962. Opened on 11 April 1962*. Received a licence from the **Red Lion**, 2 Bull Ring, which had closed in 1956. Note the logo AMB that stood for Associated Midland Brewers, a short-lived joint venture with Ansells. Pub demolished in 1992* to make way for a chemist and doctors practice where at least the pub is remembered in the name Harlequin Surgery.

TWO HANDS, Kitsland Road / Berrowside Road, Shard End, 17 April 1962. Opened on 28 March 1962. Its licence was transferred from the **Woodman**, 193/195 Sherlock Street that had closed at the end of 1957. Also carried the AMB sign. Pub still open though the flats behind are now derelict.

EDGBASTON, FIVE WAYS & LEE BANK

FIVE WAYS INN, 148 Broad Street / Ladywood Road, c. 1962 (W). You could take your pick of six doors into this large pub. However, all six doors closed forever on 29 May 1967*, for the building of the Five Ways island and Tesco supermarket.

CRUSADER, 29 Auchinleck Square / Islington Row, Five Ways. Opened 1 August 1963 within the new Five Ways Shopping Centre and is still open today. Replaced an old pub called the **Anchor** that stood on the same site at 33 Islington Row at the junction of Tennant Street. This pub had closed on 16 April 1961.

THERE'S AN **M&B** HOUSE

Quite near to you

No. 12 THE WHITE SWAN

Chad Valley, Birmingham

WHEN you visit "The White Swan" you will find the atmosphere of a country inn in the middle of a large city. It is this, together with the fact that it possesses the only skittle alley in Birmingham that accounts for its great popularity.

In summer you can enjoy an *al fresco* pint in the garden. In winter you can pep up the circulation by rolling the cheeses in the skittle alley. Whatever the season, you will find good, honest, beer, and genial company in which to drink it.

12

WHITE SWAN, 134 Harborne Road / Richmond Hill Road, 1950 (W). Its nickname is the "Dirty Duck" as once depicted on one side of its pub sign. The skittle alley has now been convert-ed into a carvery restaurant. Although in Edgbaston, the current sign intriguingly reads **Toby Carvery at Harborne.**

WOODMAN, 24 Cregoe Street / Irving Street, 1 June 1960 (W). This former Atkinson's pub is seen standing alone, awaiting demolition. It was to close for trading on 29 November 1962 and its licence was transferred to the **Pint Pot**, Emily Street, Highgate. The current **Woodman** opened 6 May 1967 at the junction with Gaywood Croft, receiving its licence from the **Shakespearian Bar**, 101 Cregoe Street.

WELCOME INN, 26 Owen Street / Wheeley's Lane c. 1948 (W). This beerhouse was granted a full licence in 1958 from the **Crown**, Leopold Street, Note the outside toilets on Owen Street. The pub closed 18 October 1964 and Owen Street has now also gone under the Bath Row Reconstruction scheme. Its licence was later transferred to the newly-built **Sir Harry**, 17 Hollies Croft (off Pershore Road) which opened for trading 10 July 1969*.

QUEEN'S STORES, 80 Bath Row / Pigott Street, 3 October 1961 (W). This beerhouse replaced an earlier one in 1908 and stood regally opposite the old Davenport's Brewery and Queen's Hospital until closure on 28 February 1962*. Its licence was transferred to the newly built **Crusader**. Both the pub and Pigott Street fell victim to the Bell Barn development, which itself is now being redeveloped.

Outdoor, 11 RICKMAN DRIVE, c. 1959 when Leonard George Egerton was the licensee. He also used to manage the nearby **Welcome Stores** outdoor at 95 Great Colmore Street. Amongst the drinks on sale were Seagers' Egg Flip, Ginger Wine and Sanatogen. Sweets available included *Rowntrees Fruit Pastilles* at 3d, *Spangles, Treats and Munchies...* not forgetting ... *Smiths potato crisps with salt*. No doubt the salt was contained in a little blue bag! Pub now closed.

TREES, 11 & 13 Bristol Road, 1 April 1961 adjacent the old Bristol cinema (replaced by a McDonalds). A former Holder's beer house that gained a full licence in 1955 and the house at no. 11 was incorporated into the pub in 1956. This charming old inn was rebuilt in 1971*.

ERDINGTON, GRAVELLY HILL, PYPE HAYES & STOCKLAND GREEN

NORTON, Kingsbury Road / Tyburn Road, c. 1948. The pub opened on 21 January 1927 and the architects were James & Lister Lea. It was to close in 2000*.

BAGOT ARMS, Chester Road & Eachelhurst Road, 1 March 1962. The pub opened on 20 November 1931 by architects Bateman & Bateman. Note the coat of arms pub sign above the car park sign. Pub still open, no doubt serving residents from the considerable number of new houses built in the Tyburn Road area in recent years.

ERDINGTON ARMS, Gravelly Hill / Slade Road, 23 August 1960. A former Atkinson's house. The roar of Spaghetti Junction was still more than ten years away when this photo was taken! Rebuilt in 1973* after a temporary building had closed. Now renamed **Armada**.

BROOKVALE, Slade Road, 1964. Opened on 23 November 1934, close to Brookvale Park. The architect was H. W. Hobbiss. No doubt a favourite of visitors to the Star Cinema (left). Pub still open.

STOCKLAND INN, Marsh Hill / Streetly Road, 12 January 1960. This view is taken from the Marsh Hill side. Opened 24 November 1924 at a cost of £22,850, the architects were Bateman & Bateman. Another pub that M & B were proud of as they produced postcards of it in the 1920s. With its distinctive stone cladding and canopies carved with patterns of oak leaves and acorns, the pub still dominates this busy junction today.

CROSS KEYS, 15 High Street / Station Road, 4 May 1961. This building dates from 1911; the architects were Wood & Kendrick. Business proved to be good as an additional women's W. C was installed in 1933! The Highclare School that can be seen (right). Pub still open, little changed today.

NEW INNS, 71/73 Summer Road, 31 January 1962. A former Holder's pub, still open today retaining the decorative "Holder's" and "Smoke Room" windows. The building to the left has now gone.

SWAN INN, 61-65 High Street / Wilton Road, 18 January 1962, showing the Good Cheer Cellars outdoor. A rather plain-looking building replaced this pleasant inn, opening 17 December 1968*.

ROYAL OAK, Marsh Lane / Short Heath Road, 6 November 1959, with Canning Furniture Removals at no. 11 (left). This beerhouse still stands opposite its more illustrious neighbour, the **Red Lion**.

RED LION, 105 Station Road / Short Heath Road, c. 1960. Opposite the **Royal Oak** (far left) is the grand looking Red Lion Hotel, dating from 1899 designed by Wood and Kendrick. The bar-front is renowned for its ornate ceramic tiling, still in tact today. Note the poster telling you to "Be a Cadbury's fruit and nut case" in the days when a bar cost a shilling (5p).

ROSE & CROWN, 294 Gravelly Lane, March 1934. A former Butler's of Wolverhampton house, with gardens and bowling green at the rear. The centre entrance was later converted to a Vintners outdoor which has now been incorporated into the pub.

LEOPARD, Jerry's Lane / Flackwell Road, 31 January 1962. Despite the difficult times, the pub opened during the War on 16 December 1940 and is still there today minus the outdoor.

HALL GREEN

COLLEGE ARMS, 976 Stratford Road / Shaftmoor Lane, (view from Shaftmoor Lane) c. 1948. The pub opened on 10 May 1913; the architects were Harrison & Cox. Still open today.

Interior view of the **College Arms**, c. 1962 shows the staircase to the function room and the entrance to the bar. All this area has been altered and refurbished since.

Interior view of the **College Arms**, c. 1962 shows the lounge. The back bar shelving still survives, but the interior has been altered considerably.

BULL'S HEAD, 1320 Stratford Road / Fox Hollies Road, c. 1962. Situated at the area known as Four Ways, this current building dates from around 1840 although an inn has stood at this spot since medieval times. Formerly a Holder's inn, it was much altered and extended in 1923. Still open today although the off-licence has been replaced by an extension to the pub.

ROBIN HOOD, Stratford Road / Shirley Road (view from Stratford Road) c. 1950. This elegant mansion in Railway Renaissance style was converted by the architect H. W. Hobbiss and opened as a pub on 16 July 1926 at the area known as Six Ways. It replaced a smaller inn on Shirley Road. Still open today as a **Toby** restaurant after extensions to the side and front and with a lodge built at the left.

THREE MAGPIES, Shirley Road / School Road, c. 1950. The pub opened on 11 November 1936, in typical style of its day. Still trading today, as the **Maggies**, a *Munster Inns* house. The pub sign depicts three magpies, one of which is drinking a pint of beer.

BALDWIN, Baldwins Lane / Newborough Road c. 1962. The pub opened on 11 December 1936; the architects were Bateman & Bateman. Still open today.

YORK, York Road / Fox Hollies Road, near the Greyhound Stadium c. 1960. The pub opened on 20 November 1931, the records stating that the *"domestic furniture was supplied by Lee Longland"* (the well known Birmingham firm based at Broad Street). Harrison & Cox were the architects. Pub still open today.

SHAFTMOOR, 280 & 282 Shaftmoor Lane / Cateswell Road, 7 March 1962. The pub opened on 22 May 1931; the architects were Wood & Kendrick. Still open today.

HANDSWORTH

CALTHORPE ARMS, 152 Wellington Road / Wood Lane, 1 June 1960 (W). The houses on the far left of the pub were demolished to make way for a beer garden and car park. This Atkinson's pub is still open today.

UPLANDS, Oxhill Road opposite Sandwell Road, c. 1950. Pub first opened its doors on 16 September 1932. The architects were Harrison and Cox. Still open today.

LORD NELSON INN, 131 Booth Street, c. 1947 (W). A beerhouse that was granted a full licence in 1954. At that time, the licensee was Major Owen Hardiker but in 1961, it passed to May Louisa Hardiker who ran it until closure in 1975*. A rather empty butcher shop, Edward Payne is seen next door at no. 133. All this area including the **Oakfield Tavern** further down at 105 Booth Street has been transformed into a green open space.

STORK HOTEL, 140 Heathfield Road / Finch Road, 6 April 1965. As can be seen, it was formerly a Butler's of Wolverhampton pub and hotel. Still open today, although no longer a hotel.

HIGHLAND TAVERN, 114 Holyhead Road, c.1920. This former Holder's pub dates from 1909. A sign in the window reads... *"motor car for hire"*. Note the weighing machine (right). Pub closed in 1979* and now demolished.

WOODMAN, 375 Holyhead Road, c. 1950. This current building replaced an earlier inn. A beer house which got its full licence in 1950. West Bromwich Albion Football Club is off to the right. The pub is still open today.

WATT TAVERN, 7 Soho Hill near junction with Claremont Road, c. 1946. A beer and wine house that which was granted a full licence in 1953. Pub closed for trading 14 May 1965* and demolished to make way for the Hockley fly-over.

ROEBUCK, 130 Soho Hill / Hamstead Road c. 1947 (W), with Mists Garage in the background. One of Henry Mitchell's pubs, still open today.

BEEHIVE, 198 Soho Hill c. 1945 (W). Note the stone beehive above the door (left) and the two workers on the roof of the factory next door. Everything still survives today and the large house on the right is now a restaurant.

IVY HOUSE, 72 Soho Road / Ivy Road c. 1945. This building replaced an earlier inn around 1892 and was purchased from Butler's of Wolverhampton by M & B on 21 March 1932. The pub still there, now renamed **Gateway to India**.

BARREL INN, 215 Soho Road / Louise Road c. 1945 (W). A beer and wine house that gained its full licence in 1949. After refurbishment in the early 1960s, the pub featured the *Tub* lounge, the *Coopers* shop and around the corner in Louise Road, the *Snug*, *Off sales* and *Pleasure Gardens*. Pub is still open.

QUEEN'S HEAD, 379 Soho Road / Queen's Head Road c. 1963 (W). Mentioned in Pigot's Directory in 1828. The pub is still open.

HARBORNE

DUKE OF YORK, 1 Lordswood Road / High Street, 1 April 1961. A former Atkinson's pub which closed in January 2002, to be replaced by housing.

Outdoor, 363 High Street, c. 1967. Adjacent the Duke of York stood this shop that had a variety of uses including in recent years a hairdresser before closure and eventual demolition in 2002.

BELL, 11 Old Church Road (W). One of Harborne's oldest and most popular pubs, little changed externally since this view was taken c. 1925. Dating from the early 19th century and probably much earlier, the pub has a village-like feel to it, with a scenic view of St. Peter's Church and the bowling green at the rear. In 1897, the Church tried to purchase the Bell for £2,040 in order to enlarge the churchyard. By then it was a Butler's Crown Brewery pub. One of the Bell's regulars for many years, Reg Shakespeare, once told the author *"the lounge used to be two separate rooms and your beer would be brought over to you by a waiter back in the 1920s and 30s"*.

SCARLET PIMPERNEL, Tennal Road / Fellows Lane, opened on 11 December 1963 receiving a licence from the **Gem Vaults**, 148 Steelhouse Lane which had closed on 23 June 1961. Pub still open.

HILLYFIELDS, Quinton Road / Cadnam Close, 18 April 1961. The pub opened on 4 December 1958* gaining a licence from the **Rose Tavern**, 159 St. Vincent Street & 80 Sherborne Street, Ladywood. Still open today.

SPORTSMAN, 19 Metchley Lane, near Alma Passage, c.1950 (W). A beer and wine house that gained its full licence in 1950. Once renowned for its gooseberry growing contests. A deceptively spacious beer garden can be found at the rear.

Pub Crawl down Harborne High Street

JUNCTION, 212 High Street / Vivian Road, April 1961 (W). This well-known landmark was rebuilt at a cost of £3,816 when opened in December 1904 and dominated the High Street. The architects were Wood & Kendrick. Extended and refurbished in 2001*, it was renamed **O'Neill's.**

VINE, 310 High Street, c. 1950 (W). This old inn was eventually replaced by a new building, which opened in July 1989.

PLOUGH, 21 & 23 High Street / Grays Road, with adjacent off-licence, Good Cheer Cellars, c. 1962 (W). A beer house that gained a full licence from the **Court Restaurant,** 184 Corporation Street in 1956. (Amazingly you can still see its name plaque at the junction with James Watt Street). The Plough is little changed externally today although much of the interior received a major refurbishment in the mid 1990s.

left
GREEN MAN, 2 High Street / Metchley Lane, 16 December 1941 (W). This current building by architect Bateman & Bateman opened 15 April 1940, replacing an older inn on the same site and is still open today.

below
STORES INN, 109 High Street / Station Road, 14 May 1965. A former private house. This beer house was granted a full licence in 1958 from the **White Swan**, 85 & 86 Legge Street, Gosta Green. Later extended and now called **Harborne Stores.**

A picture of the manager Mr. F. W. Hawkes serving Dumbarton whisky at the **Green Man**, 1953.

HIGHGATE

AUDREY ARMS, 88 Moseley Street, close to junction with Alcester Street, 27 August 1953. A former beerhouse which gained its full licence in 1921 when the pub was rebuilt. Closed in 1980* and now a trading unit occupies this site.

CARPENTERS ARMS, 1 Adelaide Street / Lower Darwin Street, 14 May 1965 (W). Replacing an earlier building, the name of the pub reflecting the dual occupation of the first licensee, this current house was opened on 20 July 1925; the architects were James & Lister Lea. Note the newly-built Rotunda in the background. Pub still open today, sporting a black and white half-timbered effect inside.

PEACOCK, 25 Darwin Street / Dymoke Street, 25 February 1965 (W). Formerly a Mitchell's pub which was substantially rebuilt in its current Neo-Regency style in 1935 at a cost of £4,175. The architect was J. B. Surman, who had taken over the practice of James & Lister Lea. Still open today, the pub stands out in a much-changed street.

ROEBUCK, 177 Darwin Street / Hollier Street, c. 1945. This charming old beerhouse was formerly a wood turner's house. Demolished 1957* to make way for new housing. Shawbury Grove has now been built on the site of Hollier Street.

BELGRAVE, Belgrave Road & 339 Moseley Road, 1945. Also showing C. P. Grimley, lamp makers at no. 341. In the 1930s, the public toilet at this pub was leased to Birmingham Corporation for £1 a year! The pub closed in November 1968 for demolition.

BEEHIVE, 101 Bissell Street, 27 August 1953 (W). This former beerhouse was once under threat of closure. Renamed the **Pig and Whistle** in 1984. Now survives as a Banks's pub, called **Catherine O'Donovan** after the licensee.

SIR CHARLES NAPIER, 210 Gooch Street / Bissell Street, 1 April 1961 (W). This Atkinson's pub is still open for trading.

WELLINGTON INN, 160 Gooch Street / Bishop Street, c. 1945 (W). A former Mitchell's pub that closed in 1991* but the building still stands ... in use as a kebab house.

ST. LUKE'S TAVERN, 33 St. Luke's Road / Vere Street, c. 1946 (W). This beerhouse's nickname was the "Bosted Boot". The pub closed on 4 November 1962 under a compulsory purchase order and the site today is near Matthew Boulton College.

HIGHGATE TAVERN, 263 Moseley Road & Conybere Street c. 1960 (W). This former Atkinson's beerhouse was granted a full licence from the **Victoria**, 193 Bristol Street in 1959. Now trading as the **Merrymaid**.

KING'S ARMS, 246 Sherlock Street / Benacre Street, 14 February 1951 (W). Next door at Seville house is E. J. Swift & Co, Wine & Spirit Merchants. Pub closed 31 October 1967 under a compulsory purchase order; its licence was later transferred to the **Grapevine**, Paradise Circus that opened for trading 15 March 1973*. All this area has been redeveloped. Benacre Street is now Mowbray Street.

BALTIC, 276 Sherlock Street & 34 Hope Street (W). Formerly a Mitchell's pub. Here we see **3 different views** showing how the pub and surrounding area has changed over the years. **Firstly** from c. 1920, with ornate lamps and mirrors in the windows. A tram stop on Sherlock Street advises "for cars to city".

Secondly from c. 1945, the windows have been boarded up no doubt due to the war; the ornate lamps have gone but a lamp standard has appeared on the tram wire pole. An additional window has appeared on the first floor.

Finally from 1965, the Baltic name only appears in small lettering; the trams have gone and a no waiting road sign appears instead of the lamppost and the wall next door to the newsagent has gone. Closed 26 May 1968 for demolition under what M & B called the *Gooch Street Reconstruction Area* scheme.

HOCKLEY & JEWELLERY QUARTER

HEN & CHICKENS, 27 Constitution Hill / Henrietta Street, c. 1960 (W). Mentioned in Pigot's Directory in 1828. A former Atkinson's pub, distinctive in style, still open today.

GOTHIC, 1 Great Hampton Street / Great Hampton Row, 1 September 1961. Dating from around 1900, built in distinctive Gothic style, this fine building, typical of many in the area, stands three storeys high. With nearly fifty windows and with decorative brickwork over the arches, this must have been a good day's work for the local window cleaner! Sadly the pub closed in 1991* and the future is uncertain for this magnificent building.

MINERVA VAULTS, 17 Great Hampton Row / Mott Street, c. 1964 (W). A former Atkinson's pub, dating from around 1825, now sporting a black and white half-timbered look. During World War Two a bomb fell down the chimney of the house opposite and the Minerva took the full force of the blast. All the windows were blown out, killing both customers in the bar and the firewatchers standing outside. The factory behind has now been replaced by a trading estate and the pub has been renamed the **Great Hampton**.

WHITE HORSE CELLARS, 106 Constitution Hill / Northwood Street, c. 1930 (W). Listed in Pigot's Directory of Birmingham in 1829, the current building was a rebuild by James & Lister Lea. In 2000* the pub sadly closed, but may reopen as a restaurant.

A view of the public toilet that stood adjacent the **White Horse Cellars** by the railway bridge, 1979. Seen here in a state of disrepair, it was later demolished.

RAILWAY TAVERN, 292 Park Road / Norton Street, c. 1920 (W) seen here after recent alterations. A new purchase for M & B on 27 February 1917, the pub is still open, little changed externally today.

RED LION, 95 Warstone Lane, c. 1930 (W). Later became a Banks's house, still open.

LORD CLIFDEN, 34 Great Hampton Street, 11 September 1961 (W). Dating from the early 1800s, this former Holder's beer house gained a full licence in 1952. It was rebuilt after a fire in 1921 and further alterations were carried out in the 1930s. M & B leased out the building that stands behind, at this time to W.F. Hadley, machinists. The pub is still open. Note the superb Lord Clifden stained glass window.

JEWELLERS' ARMS, 23 Hockley Street / Spencer Street, 31 January 1957. Formerly a Mitchell's pub called the **Goldsmiths' and Jewellers' Arms**, its name reflecting the predominant trade in this area and although once threatened with closure it still forms part of Birmingham's Jewellery Quarter today.

DUKE OF YORK, 16 Hockley Hill / Key Hill, c. 1965 (W: as **Old Tree Inn**). A splendid Georgian building. The coffee shop at 60 Key Hill belonged to the pub. There is still a cafe is here today but the pub sadly closed in 1996*, and in June of that year the distinctive back bar with the heading "Champagne, Irish and Scotch Whiskey, Wines and Spirits" was stolen.

ROSE VILLA TAVERN, 172 Warstone Lane / Vyse Street, c. 1962 (W). Dating from 1919-1920 and designed by architect Wood & Kendrick, it was built at the high cost of £15,000, replacing an earlier tavern. At the heart of the Jewellery Quarter, by the Chamberlain Memorial Clock, this pub still retains many splendid original features including coloured stained glass windows and plenty of tiles and tile-painting.

GEORGE & DRAGON, 12 Albion Street / Carver Street, c. 1960. Dating from c. 1870 this is a Grade II listed building originally built for the independent brewer Matthew Bower. The pub was attached to the George & Dragon Brewery in Pope Street. The brewery building was sold in 1936. It is sad to see this interesting Victorian pub now closed. In January 1997, the distinctive wooden seating, glass roundels and George and Dragon motifs were stolen.

QUEEN'S HEAD, 1 Burbury Street / Bridge Street West, 6 September 1960. This Atkinson's pub stood opposite Joseph Lucas Ltd, Great King Street. Closed 4 June 1969* and now demolished.

PUB CRAWL DOWN ICKNIELD STREET

The following five pubs were all located on the west side of Icknield Street running from Spring Hill up towards Hockley Hill. They were all demolished in the early 1970s due to the road widening and upgrading of the street as part of the Middle Ring Road. Many other nearby pubs in the Hockley / Winson Green area were also lost.

WARSTONE, 168 Icknield Street / Camden Street, c. 1965 (W). An Atkinson's beerhouse. Closed for trading 28 September 1971* and its licence transferred to the **Florin** (opened on 1 February 1974*) which has also now closed.

ROYAL MINT, 200 Icknield Street & 1 Hingeston Street, c. 1962. An Atkinson's pub, handy for the number 8 bus and also for Birmingham's Royal Mint over the road. A decree from the Licensing Court in 1925 said that *"drinking be discouraged and as far as possible prevented in the passage entrance hall off Icknield Street"*. Closed for trading 27 September 1970*.

GATE, 183 Icknield Street / Alfred's Place, c. 1965 (W). This distinctive building dated from 1888 by architects James & Lister Lea, replacing an earlier inn. Formerly owned by Henry Mitchell. By the time of this photograph, it had lost its distinctive turret (see outside back cover). Closed for trading 25 August 1970*.

ROYAL OAK, 210 Icknield Street / Great Western Terrace, c. 1935 when John Adkins was the licensee (W). An old beerhouse whose licensee in 1869 was also a grocer! Closed for trading 1970*.

GREAT WESTERN INN, 241 Icknield Street / Park Road, 1970 (W). As reflected in its name, this pub stood near to Hockley railway station which itself closed in 1972. It is seen here awaiting demolition after it had closed for trading on 15 July 1970*. The **Abbey Vaults** pub can be seen in the distance down Park Road (far left).

ABBEY VAULTS, 31 Lodge Road / Park Road, 1 June 1960 (W). Its nickname was the "Wrexham". This former Atkinson's pub closed for trading 17 January 1971*. Norfolk Tower flats now stands behind where the pub stood. Park Road no longer meets Lodge Road at this junction.

HYDRAULIC, 356 Lodge Road / All Saints' Street, c. 1962. Another Atkinson's house, popular with the workers of Scibbans's bakers over the road. Closed in 1970* and housing now occupies this site.

ROYAL EXCHANGE, 152 Park Road, c. 1930. This beer house was granted a full licence in 1963. Closed for trading 1 March 1970*. The pub and this row of shops have now been demolished.

KING'S HEATH, MOSELEY & YARDLEY WOOD

RED LION, 229 Vicarage Road / Grove Road, c. 1950. Opened 11 August 1904 at a cost of £5,381/18/5! The architect was C. E. Bateman and front of the building was finished in Wildon stone. It was the first of a new type of reformed, large, separate public house, which later came into their own in the 1920s and 30s. This "religious building" style was a deliberate attempt to make drinking in pubs a respectable past time. It features carvings of monks quaffing brimming tankards of ale. The pub is still open today and thrives as a live music venue.

CROSS GUNS (old building), 70 High Street / Bank Street c. 1910. The sign outside says that the hotel as it was then, dates from 1792.

CROSS GUNS (new building), 21 March 1962. The current building dates from c. 1924. Now renamed the **Goose and Granite**.

KINGS ARMS, 290 Alcester Road South, 27 February 1958. This former Holder's house was rebuilt back in 1911 by William Jenkins, architect. A twin bus shelter shelters some people as they await the 48 or 50 into the city centre. The pub, nicknamed the "Nob" is still open today.

HORSE SHOE INN, 611 Alcester Road South, 8 March 1962. Close to the Stratford-upon-Avon canal, the road that this pub stood on used to be called Millpool Hill until renamed in 1927. Pub still open today.

MAYPOLE, Alcester Road South / Maypole Lane, c. 1936. Everything was new on this postcard showing the newly built Maypole, which opened 17 July 1936; the architect was J. A. Harper. The two Daimler buses were new in 1935. The bus routes were old however; this was before the current no. 50. The first bus showing the route "Chester Road Erdington 17" ran northwards and the other bus ran showing the route "Alcester Road Maypole 35" southwards. In the summer of 2002 the pub closed; the area to become dominated by a supermarket.

Outdoor, 4 Albert Road, c. 1957 when Mrs. Mabel Gladys Hill was the licensee. A sign in the window urges you to "buy Bulmer's cider inside."

MOSELEY

COVERED WAGON, 298 Yardley Wood Road, c. 1963. This pub opened on 17 October 1962 replacing an outdoor which had been operating since 9 February 1927. It received its licence from the **Dolphin**, Unett Street that had closed in 1957. Note the fine pub sign. Pub still open today.

HIGHBURY, Moor Green Lane / Dads Lane, 8 March 1962. The first licensee is recorded as H. E. Woolaston in July 1929. Still in business today.

YARDLEY WOOD

HAVEN, School Road near Chilton Road, c. 1962, with the "Captain's Room" (left) and "Harbour Lounge Ward Room" (right). This pub, built in 1929, was by H. W. Hobbiss and featured a half-timbered look with red and blue brick. The stone plaques denoted a ship and a windmill. Certainly a windmill did used to stand in the vicinity. Later renamed the **Old Cottage**, its licence was revoked in 1997* and has now been demolished to make way for a health centre, although the cobbled driveway has survived.

BAGNELL ARMS, School Road / Warstock Lane, c. 1962. This building opened on 17 May 1960 receiving a licence from the **White Hart**, 41 Cromwell Street, Bloomsbury. Closed in 2001*.

VALLEY, Yardley Wood Road / Haunch Lane, 7 March 1962. The pub opened on 21 January 1927 near to the Happy Valley beauty spot and was another of M & B's showcase pubs by Wood & Kendrick. However it eventually developed structural problems and closed in 1996*. Appartments now occupy this large site.

Here we see the interior view of the Smoke Room of the **Valley** as it was in 1929.

KING'S NORTON, COTTERIDGE & STIRCHLEY

BULL'S HEAD, 75 & 77 The Green, June 1964, The pub was rebuilt in 1901 by architects James & Lister Lea. Note the parish church (right), giving the area a village feel to it. Three neighbouring houses owned by M & B were demolished in 1955. The **Saracen's Head**, at no. 55 had closed for trading on 15 May 1930 and was gifted to Kings Norton Parish Church on 2 September 1930. Today it serves as the Parish Office. The **Bull's Head** still thrives today as it did when King's Norton was a village in Worcestershire!

CARTLAND ARMS, Broad Meadow Lane / Parson's Hill, 18 January 1962. Opened 19 November 1937 having been planned 13 years earlier and originally its name was to be the **Broadmeadow**. The architects were Wood & Kendrick. In 1987* it was renamed the **Sporting Parson**, and by 1997* it was trading as **Poacher's Pocket.** It is no longer a pub but the building is now in use as a McDonalds restaurant which opened in December 2000.

LONGBOW, Greaves Square, Pool Farm, Walker's Heath, c. 1966. First opened 21 April 1966; receiving a licence from the **Railway**, Great Francis Street (see under Nechells) featuring the *Arden* Lounge and *Longbow* Bar. No longer a pub since 1992*, the building is currently occupied by an aquatic supply centre.

HAZELWELL, Pineapple Road / Hazelwell Fordrough, 12 May 1961. Dating from 1931, the architects were Bateman & Bateman. The pub is still open, little changed externally today.

GRANT ARMS, 1814 Pershore Road / Cotteridge Road, Cotteridge, 21 March 1962. Opened for trading on 16 May 1930; the architects were Wood & Kendrick. The pub is still open.

BRITISH OAK, 1364 Pershore Road, Stirchley c. 1960. New building opened 17 September 1926 replacing an earlier inn. A typical example of Birmingham's new pubs of the 1920s that looks a bit out of place in this tight spot. Set back from the road for ease of parking, there is also a terrace and a bowling green. The architect was Mr. Brassington of James & Lister Lea, who also designed the **Barton's Arms**. Pub still open, boasting many original features.

The Assembly Room, **British Oak**, as it looked in 1929 with the tables set for shilling dinners.

LADYWOOD

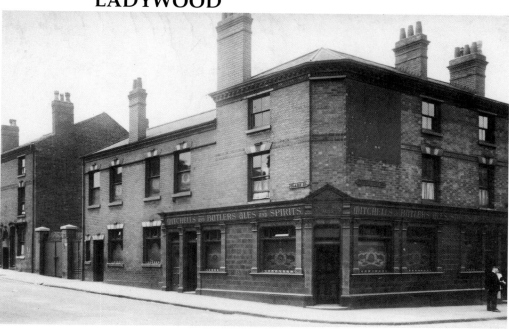

GLASSBLOWERS ARMS, 41 Icknield Port Road / Clark Street, c. 1946. Also shows property that M & B owned at 2 and 4 Clark Street. A former Holder's beer-house that gained its full licence in 1922. No doubt this pub was a local for the glassmakers of nearby Freeth Street, but the pub which closed in 1968* has now gone as indeed have so many of old Ladywood 's old pubs.

FREETH ARMS, 314 Icknield Port Road / Freeth Street, 6 September 1960 (W). A former Atkinson's pub that was to close in 1967*. Maybe the three lads by the Zebra Crossing were discussing what a great song "Apache" by the Shadows was, number one in the hit parade when this photo was taken. Nowadays, though, there is just green and pleasant "wonderful" land where this pub once stood

HYDE ARMS, 80 Hyde Road & 41 Clark Street, c. 1946. An old local that was extensively altered in 1935. At one stage M & B owned the shop (left), before Birmingham Corporation bought it in 1952. Closed 3 November 1968 and this part of Hyde Road has now disappeared.

RESERVOIR INN, 132 Osler Street / Reservoir Road, c. 1920 (W). After an early 1960s refurbishment, the Reservoir Road entrance (left) featured *The Lake Side* and *Off Sales* and Osler Street entrance (right) led you to the *Silver Birch* lounge. The sign above the door to the bar on this photo reads: "William Edward Jeavons, Licensed Retailer of foreign wines & spirits, ale, porter, cider & tobacco..." Alas even with this fine display of alcoholic refreshment the pub closed on 6 February 1968* as Osler Street was redeveloped. In 1975 its licence went to a new pub in Kings Norton, the **King's Oak**, Vardon Way.

NAG'S HEAD, 298 Monument Road / Icknield Port Road, c. 1946 (W). One of Ladywood's beerhouses which survived until 1968* near to the swimming baths but alas all these buildings have now gone.

TURF, 434 & 435 Monument Road / Spring Hill, c. 1965 (W). A former Atkinson's pub, with distinctive neon sign. When this photo was taken, there appears to be two smoke rooms, one on the left in Monument Road and one on the right in Spring Hill! Closed for demolition 9 January 1967* and Ladywood Middleway replaced this part of Monument Road.

RYLAND ARMS, 33 & 35 Ryland Street, c.1946 (W). Formerly a Mitchell's pub situated just off Broad Street. The architect H. W. Hobbiss carried out alterations in 1935. Closed on 20 May 1962 under a compulsory purchase order and flats now occupy this site. Amazingly the cobbled street still survives!

VINE INN, 133 King Edward's Road / Garbett Street, c.1925 (W). Another humble beerhouse, boasting a highly ornate spherical lamp. Not to be confused with the former Ansells pub of the same name that still stands in Rawlins Street. Closed in 1968* and again, no trace of this pub remains today.

JUSTICE HOUSE, Outdoor, 55 St. Mark's Street / King Edward's Road, 25 April 1962, by which time it was run by Mrs. Vera Cartledge. It closed on 18 September 1963.

IVY GREEN, 22 Edward Street & 15 Clement Street, 9 November 1961 (W). Note the dual address of this Henry Mitchell pub. Many of the surrounding houses went to the council under a compulsory purchase order. The pub itself closed in 1969* for redevelopment.

BRIDGE INN, 73 Monument Road, c.1965. Another Henry Mitchell pub that stood opposite Monument Lane railway station, which had already closed to passenger traffic in 1958. You can just see the wonderful Victorian gentleman's toilet complete with gas lamp (left). The pub closed for redevelopment of the site on 29 March 1967.

CUP STORES, **Outdoor**, 21 Ruston Street, c.1946. Typical of many such off-licences in the area, at this time ran by Mary Ann Eccles but now demolished.

ST. VINCENT, St. Vincent Street West. Interior view showing the lounge taken not long after the pub opened on 21 March 1967, its licence coming from the **Royal Oak**, 92/93 Great Lister Street. Still going strong today.

PIED PIPER, Ledsam Street. This pub opened on 17 February 1967, receiving a licence from the soon-to-be-closed **Bridge** at Monument Road. No longer in use as a pub and in 1999* the building was converted into offices of the UK Confucian Society.

COMMERCIAL INN, 28 Shakespeare Road / Anderton Street, c. 1965. A sign promoting "Pies" hangs in the doorway of the Outdoor (left). This old beer and wine house gained a full licence in 1957 from the closed **Shakespeare Inn,** 87 St. Mark's Street but was to close itself on 30 May 1968 for redevelopment. Shakespeare Road has gone completely as has this part of Anderton Street. St. Mark's Crescent is approximately on this site today.

OLD ROBIN HOOD, 101 Garbett Street / Summer Hill Street, 25 May 1965 (W). A former Butler's of Wolverhampton beerhouse. Note the outside Gentleman's toilet (left). Closed in 1967*. Garbett Street has also disappeared and this site is approximately where the Nelson primary school is today.

KING EDWARD STORES, 49 Nelson Street & King Edward's Road, c. 1946. This beerhouse was granted a full licence in 1957 when the licence of the **Clock Tavern,** Ashted Row was surrendered. Closed 2 March 1966, under a compulsory purchase order. Like the **Robin Hood,** today the Nelson school now occupies this site.

For more Ladywood pubs, see *"Stop Press"* on page 138.

LOZELLS

BELLE VUE INN, 276 Wheeler Street / 101 Gerrard Street, c. 1946 (W). M & B leased the shop next door, to the Lozells Motor Company at the time. A former Holder's house which closed in 1969*. Again all these buildings have gone, but at least the nearby **Gunmakers' Arms** at 123 Gerrard Street has survived.

ROSE & CROWN, 318 Wheeler Street / Gower Street, c. 1962 (W). This former Henry Mitchell's pub closed in 1969* for demolition.

UNION INN, 146 Berners Street / Gerrard Street, c. 1926 (W). This Holder's beerhouse was granted a full licence in 1951. Note the horse-drawn Norton Street Baker's van. The pub is still open.

NEW INNS, 172 Berners Street, May Day 1904 (W). A superb photo of the M & B horse-drawn wagon outside the pub, which closed many years ago in 1927*.

ACORN INN, 185 Wheeler Street & 80 Wilton Street, c. 1948 (W). Formerly a Holder's house. The door on the left led to the out-door department, with a small bar room attached. The main entrance led into a long sloping passage that came out in the next street hence the dual address. As well as the main bar, small bar, and Smoke room, a staircase in the passage led up to the Assembly rooms which included the landlord's living accommodation, a concert room with seating for 200 people and artistes dressing rooms. The Acorn was famous back in the 1930s for its " Free and Easy " nights. One of the artistes who performed there, Cecil Hayes, liked the pub so much, he became the licensee! The late Denis Howell M.P started his career speaking at a political meeting at the Assembly Room at the age of 17. Note the superb glasswork, a feature of this pub. Closed 26 September 1968* and now no trace of the pub now remains.

OBSERVATORY INN, 44A Barker Street / Hunter's Road, c. 1945 (W), photo taken from the Barker Street side. A charming surviving example of a small back street beerhouse in an "olde worlde" part of Lozells, close to Villa Cross, Handsworth. A former Holder's house. Even the old paving blocks in Hunter's Road are still in tact! The pub was promoted to receive a full licence in 1949.

BELL INN, 60 Lozells Road, near to junction with Wilton Street, c 1962 (W). In the early 1900s, there was a billiards room where pool and pyramids (the forerunners of snooker) were played. Concerts and Debating Society meetings were also held here. The house next door at no. 58 became a Good Cheer Cellars off-licence in 1958. The pub is still open today but the **Lozells Inn** that stands opposite at no. 67/69 has now closed.

ANGEL, 81 George Street / Wills Street, c. 1962 (W: as Angel Hotel). This Atkinson's beer house ceased trading as a pub in 1995* but the building is still in use as offices.

WATERLOO STORES, 37 Wills Street, 22 May 2002. A former beerhouse that gained a full licence in 1952 but its licence was not renewed in 2001*. An example of the many old pubs in Birmingham that are closed and are sadly falling into disrepair.

NECHELLS, ASHTED, DUDDESTON, VAUXHALL & BLOOMSBURY

PRINCE OF WALES, 72 Long Acre / Thimble Mill Lane, c. 1964 (W). This former Atkinson's pub was sold to Birmingham's Highway Department in 1992* for road widening and improvement.

WOODMAN, 39 Cattell's Grove / Johnson Street, 21 June 1965 (W). This former Butler's of Wolverhampton beerhouse closed 29 June 1975* to be replaced by housing.

SPORTSMAN, 130 Saltley Road, 16 February 1962 (W). M & B bought this pub along with the property next door at no. 128 in 1919. However no. 128 was bombed during the last War and had to be demolished. M & B then sold the land to the Brock Metal Co. whose factory can be seen either side of the Sportsman. The pub is still open today.

JENNY LIND, 62 Aston Church Road / Mount Street, c. 1925 (W). A typical example of a back street pub prevalent in the Nechells area. Named after the Swedish-born singer extremely popular in Victorian times. It was to close in 1940*.

SOLDIER'S RETURN, 158 Nechells Park Road, June 1975 (W). The first licensee was recorded in 1856, so the name could have been a reference to the Crimean War. A beerhouse that gained a full licence in 1959 from the **Wheatsheaf**, 138 Latimer Street, Lee Bank. Note the superb Co-Op shop front next door, which dated from 1905 and seemingly little changed since. Bargains included Coca-Cola at 9½p, Cream Crackers at 10p and Kellogg's Rice Crispies at 31p. Pub closed 6 April 1975* and both these buildings have now gone since this area was rebuilt.

ROYAL EXCHANGE, 222 Rocky Lane / Long Acre, c. 1933. This pub closed on 31 October 1954 and all of this area has been rebuilt. Long Acre no longer meets Rocky Lane.

BREWERY TAVERN, 209 Bloomsbury Street / Cranbury Street, c. 1946 (W). This old beerhouse gained a full licence in 1958 from the **Castle & Falcon**, 109 Digbeth. Closed 6 September 1967 under a compulsory purchase order, as this area was cleared for high rise flat development.

RAILWAY INN, 148/9 Great Francis Street / Claverdon Street, c. 1948 (W). This beerhouse closed on 15 July 1954* as this area was an early target of the slum clearance policy.

DOG & PARTRIDGE, 51/52 Ashted Row & 128 Windsor Street, c. 1962 (W). The pub is still there but Ashted Row is now the dual carriageway, Nechells Parkway. The pub still bears the Ashted Row street sign. One of the area's oldest pubs, dating from the late 1700's.

VICTORIA INN, 99 Duddeston Mill Road / Inkerman Street, 16 February 1962 (W). Closed for demolition 14 June 1976*. This is now the site of Vauxhall Trading Estate.

BLACK HORSE, 222 Ashted Row / Woodcock Street, c. 1925 (W). One of William Butler's pubs before he joined forces with Henry Mitchell when the beer was supplied from The Crown, Broad Street. Typical example of the style of pub rebuilt by architects James & Lister Lea. Pub still open (although the address has changed to 22 Jennens Road). An interesting back bar still remains inside, with a mirror engraved with the date 1846.

MANOR ARMS, 1 Cato Street / Duddeston Mill Road, c. 1962. This beerhouse gained a full licence from the **Three Horseshoes**, Catherine Street in 1957. The adjoining houses either side of the Manor Arms were merged into the pub in 1951. Pub closed 8 June 1975*. An industrial unit has now replaced the pub.

ASHTED HAMLET, Vauxhall Road, Nechells Green, c. 1966. The pub opened on 13 September 1966; its licence came from the **Swan** at nearby Loxton Street. The off-licence is advertising "4 shillings (20p) off spirits and 2 shillings (10p) off wines." However the pub had a relatively short life as it closed in 1997*. Its near neighbour, the **Rocket**, Great Francis Street has faired better, still open for business.

JUNCTION STORES, Outdoor, 176 Long Acre / Stuart Street, 20 August 1959 when Doreen Ada Brindle was the licensee. Looking like a mini pub, the outdoor was to close on 28 February 1965 and the site is now a school play area.

ALBION VAULTS, 73 Cato Street North / Nechells Place, 21 June 1965 (W). Known locally as *Peggy's* or *Roper's,* after the long-standing landlady who retired in 2002 after thirty years! This former Butler's local is still open.

NEWTOWN, SUMMER LANE & NEW TOWN ROW

BROOK TAVERN, 53 Lennox Street, 17 November 1966. This beerhouse gained its full licence in 1952. The pub was to close on 21 April 1968 for eventual demolition and redevelopment.

DUKE OF CAMBRIDGE, 150/151 Great King Street / Berners Street, c. 1930 (W). This old building was subsequently knocked down and a new pub opened on 23 July 1937. Even this replacement closed in 1993* due to the widespread redevelopment of the area. The lower end of Berners Street has gone and the site is approximately where Orchid Drive is today.

ST. MATTHIAS TAVERN, 199 Great Russell Street / Bridge Street West, c. 1946 (W). Dating from the 1880s, an extension was later added (left) to the original building. This beerhouse was granted a full licence in 1954. Closed for demolition in 1968*. Great Russell Street no longer exists and the site is open green space today.

WHITE SWAN, 356 Farm Street / Villa Street, 11 September 1961 (W). This beerhouse gained its full licence in 1952. The pub closed on 23 March 1966 under a compulsory purchase order for redevelopment.

ROSE & CROWN, 154 Brearley Street / Hospital Street, c.1946 (W). After some bomb damage in 1941, neighbours recalled how the beer was rescued after the dust had settled and taken into nearby houses for safekeeping so that there was something left to celebrate the "all clear" with. In 1957 six locals were fined £1 each for drinking out of permitted hours. Demolition had already started in this area when this photo was taken and this beerhouse was to close on 20 September 1963. A new street, Aldgate Grove today lies approximately on this site.

SPORTSMAN, 202 New Town Row / Moorsom Street, c. 1946 (W). The house, left, at no. 200 was absorbed into the pub in 1929. In 1957 this beerhouse gained a full licence which had been surrendered from the **White Lion**, 84 New Town Row. Pub survived until 1973* and was subsequently demolished.

PUB CRAWL DOWN SUMMER LANE

STAG'S HEAD, 79 & 80 Summer Lane / Brearley Street, c. 1930 (W). The pub dates from the 1830s. Used to have a "men's only" bar although women were allowed in a screened off portion of the bar, but they wouldn't be served. No such problems today and the pub still thrives.

GREEN MAN, 141 Summer Lane / Moorsom Street, c. 1946 (W). This former Holder's beerhouse closed on 4 March 1965 when this end of Moorsom Street was demolished.

WOODMAN, 198 Summer Lane/ Asylum Road, 1 June 1960 (W). A former Atkinson's pub also known locally as the Wrexham, possibly because Wrexham ales were sold there. Closed 13 May 1962 when the pub and Asylum Road was swept away. Site now occupied by Newtown Shopping Centre.

BIRMINGHAM HOUSE, 243 Summer Lane / Farm Street, 11 September 1961 (W). A well-patronised pub in its heyday. A local reminisces about the bar: "*a stove stood in the middle of the room which would glow red hot at times... There was always clean sawdust down, with polished brass spittoons dotted around... The first door in Farm Street was the outdoor where there were a few stools provided for the ones that wanted a quick drink in privacy... the second door was the Smoke room where there were highly polished tables and stools, with high-backed benches around the walls, upholstered in plush velvet...* " Dating from 1865, this pub was bombed in the War but still survived closure until 7 March 1968. The pub along with this part of Farm Street was demolished.

BRITANNIA INN, 286 Summer Lane / New John Street West, c. 1925 (W). The first recorded manager dated from 1831. A nearby house at no. 287 was later absorbed into the pub. Had a reputation as a well-run pub, no doubt due to it being the local of the nearby Bridge Street West police station! The pub closed 2 March 1961 for demolition.

ROYAL GEORGE, 350 Summer Lane / William Street North, c. 1930 (W). The shop next door shows off an impressive array of enamel signs! The pub is still open today; having been renamed the **Olde Lane** and the Victorian William Street North street sign has also still survived.

GLOBE, 35 Blews Street / Manchester Street, 21 June 1965. Dating back to the 1830s; formerly a Fred Smith's house, later taken over by William Butler of Wolverhampton. Pub still open.

Outdoor, 56 Geach Street / Rodway Street, 12 November 1966 when Ronald William Perrott was the licensee. This building and Rodway Street have now gone, replaced by housing.

LORD BYRON, 124 Farm Street / Well Street c. 1930 (W), with Joseph Lucas's receiving depot nearby. This Holder's beer house gained a full licence in 1949. Closed for trading 1993*. Everything in this scene has now gone.

NORTHFIELD, LONGBRIDGE, WEST HEATH, TURVES GREEN, REDNAL & RUBERY

TRAVELLERS' REST, Bristol Road South / Bell Lane, c. 1926. This distinctive pub complete with thatched roof was designed by architects Bateman & Bateman and opened 21 May 1926, replacing an earlier beerhouse. However, a fire on 14 July 1941 destroyed the roof and the pub was closed until 21 November for rebuilding. An off-licence was added (far left) in 1954. Still open today but under threat due to a road-widening scheme.

GREAT STONE INN, 158 Church Road / Church Hill, 8 March 1962. By this time the stone from which the pub took its name had been moved next door in the village pound for safe keeping. Stray animals were kept in the village pound until their owner had paid the appropriate fee. Pub still open.

BEECHES, Merritts Brook Lane / Basil Road, on a postcard issued by M & B c.1933. The architect was Ewen Harper and the pub opened on 20 January 1933. Still open today.

KING GEORGE V, Bristol Road South / Tessall Lane, 27 February 1958. The pub opened on 20 January 1937, having been planned twelve years earlier. One of the last pubs by architects James & Lister Lea before they concentrated on their estate agency business. Having survived an earlier closure attempt, the pub closed in the summer of 2002 for conversion into a restaurant.

COCK INN, Rubery Lane, Rubery, c. 1962. The bowling green was built in 1921. Not so much a country pub today, now that this area has been extensively built up.

JOLLY FITTER, Longbridge Lane / Turves Green, 19 December 1958. Pub opened 21 November 1958, no doubt taking its name from the nearby car assembly plant at Longbridge. Received a licence from the **Red Lion**, 33 Smallbrook Street, a pub that had suffered bomb damage. Still open today.

WOODPECKER, The Oak Walk / Turves Green, 26 January 1962. The pub opened 20 December 1961 receiving a licence from the **Swan with Two Necks**, 12 Lawley Street. Still open today under the Sizzling Pub Co. banner.

LONGBRIDGE, 1836 Bristol Road South / Ashill Road, c. 1950. This pub was opened on 4 March 1932 and the architect was S. N. Cooke. It occupied a large site of 6000 square yards. No doubt this proved irresistible to the planners as the licence of the **"Bridge"** was surrendered 14 December 1995* and the pub was demolished to make way for housing.

MAN IN THE MOON, 609 Redditch Road / Redhill Road, West Heath, c. 1937. First opened 15 October 1937, the architect was Bateman & Bateman. As was common with similarly named pubs, its name was changed to Man *on* the Moon on 20 July 1969 to commemorate the moon landing. Pub still open.

Outdoor, 324 Old Birmingham Road, Rednal, 26 September 1962 when Elizabeth Riches was the licensee.

PERRY BARR, KINGSTANDING & OSCOTT

TENNIS COURT, Walsall Road near Church Road, 1 February 1962. Plans to build a pub on this site near Perry Park were drawn up as far back as January 1931 by the architect Hobbiss; it was originally planned to be called the Hand & Racquet. The slightly more catchy tennis theme prevailed and eventually it opened on 18 December 1939. Still open today.

TOWERS, 636 Walsall Road near Dyas Avenue, c. 1950. The Towers reflects the area within Perry Barr known as Tower Hill, the site of an old farm. In the 1930s, housing grew rapidly in this area and the new pub was opened on 22 May 1936. Architects were Wood & Kendrick. Today it is a Sizzling Pub Co. bar and restaurant.

DRAKE'S DRUM, Old Oscott Lane / Aldridge Road, c. 1945. The pub opened 20 May 1940; the architects were the Birmingham firm of John Alfred Harper. Still open; close to North Birmingham College.

GOLDEN HIND, 188 Kingstanding Road / Greenholm Road, c. 1948. Complete with a mock Tudor effect, the Golden Hind opened on 18 November 1938; the architects were Scott & Clark. Pub is still open today.

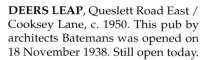

DEERS LEAP, Queslett Road East / Cooksey Lane, c. 1950. This pub by architects Batemans was opened on 18 November 1938. Still open today.

REST AND BE THANKFUL 20 Cooksey Lane near junction with Norbury Road, 25 May 1959. The pub had opened for exactly two months when this view was taken, receiving a licence from the **Hope & Anchor**, 79 Caroline Street. Still open today, now called the **Sportsman's Rest**.

KING'S STANDING, King's Road / Kingstanding Road c. 1966. Opened 26 September 1966, replacing an earlier building that had opened on 6 October 1933 and closed in 1965. Since then, to the regret of many of the regulars, this distinctive three-storey building was again replaced by the current plain building in 1989. The Top Rank Club (far right) still survives in use as a bingo club.

HARE & HOUNDS, 413 Kingstanding Road, 4 May 1961. Opened in 1931*. Later renamed **Kings** and currently known as the **Pudding and Pint**.

THE STORES, Outdoor, 250 Chester Road North, New Oscott, 18 November 1960 when Reginald Arthur Boyles kept this Atkinson's off-licence. It was later knocked down and replaced with flats.

CHASE, Parkhouse Drive, Wyrley Birch Estate, Perry Common, c. 1965. Opened 2 March 1965; its licence coming from the **Black Lion**, 20 Smallbrook Street. A typical 1960s pub by architects Forshaw, Greaves & Parkes. Still open today, now called **Ridgeway Arms**.

QUINTON, WOODGATE & BARTLEY GREEN

BEECH TREE, 321 Hagley Road West / Wolverhampton Road South, c. 1910. This old inn, typical of its time (early 1800s) shows the licensee Mr. & Mrs. Peace and family. This building was later replaced by the current larger house and was renamed the **Bass House**, 18 July 1968* by which time the pub was under Bass administration. After further refurbishment it was renamed **Amber Tavern**.

PUNCHBOWL, 153 Wolverhampton Road South / Ridgacre Road, c. 1955. The pub opened on 15 October 1937 built on land purchased from the owner of nearby Redhall farm. The pub contained some interesting features such as a number of fine stained glass windows depicting William Shenstone and Halesowen Abbey among others. Its name came from the seventeenth hole on the golf course, opposite, where the Quinborne Library and Community Centre now stands. Pub still open.

Mr. Charlie Hill, manager of the **Punchbowl**, tending the cellar, 1953. Rumour has it that his ghost still haunts the premises to this day!

NEW INN, Ridgacre Road West c. 1910. Seen here when still owned by Cheshire's brewery of Smethwick. Remembered with great fondness by the locals for its ox roasts and outside horse troughs, it eventually closed and its licence transferred to the newly opened, larger **King's Highway** in 1940.

HOLLY BUSH, Hagley Road West / Quinton Lane, 14 April 1961. This building dates from 1937 and replaced a smaller inn located further up Hollybush Hill towards the Bass House. It became a **Jefferson's** restaurant from 1988* and in 2001* after further rebuilding, a **Toby** carvery, but at least the Holly Bush name has been reinstated.

Mr. Jasper Edgar Townsend, manager of the **Holly Bush** from 1941-1954, serving pints for the locals in 1953.

GOLDEN CUP, Ridgacre Road / Quinton Road West, 25 February 1965. Opened on 14 September 1955 receiving a licence from the **Bridge Tavern**, 273 Gooch Street. Typical of the more functional, less imposing design favoured by Scott & Clark, (architects) at the time. Still open today.

M & B
HOUSES

No. 29 "THE KING'S HIGHWAY"

QUINTON

THE latest of the group of " Fewer and Better " houses erected by the Company in the pre-war years, " The Kings Highway " was not completed until 1940. At the time there was some doubt as to whether it would be called up for National Service immediately upon completion, but fortunately it was decided that the work of dispensing comfort and good cheer, through the medium of " Good Honest Beer " was in itself a most essential form of National Service in those bleak days of 1940. Accordingly it was allowed to open its doors on 23rd December, just in time for Christmas.

The King's Highway stands high on the Quinton Ridge, 730 feet above sea level. It stands equally high in the good opinions of the surrounding residents, and they come, not only from Quinton itself, but also from the Black Country, to make use of the superb amenities provided. The fact that the Assembly Room is booked up night after night for months ahead is sufficient evidence of the quality of the service provided.

12

KING'S HIGHWAY, Hagley Road West / Kingsway, (Deerstalker Magazine 1953). Still open today under the Arena banner.

STAG & THREE HORSESHOES, Halesowen Road / Kent Road, c. 1937. This building opened 23 July 1937 replacing a smaller inn. Architect was Scott & Clark. Note the White Coffee house, prior to demolition for completion of the car park, entrance and road widening of Kent Road. The prolific house building in Quinton came to a halt during the War, but pubs all over Birmingham would act as meeting houses to discuss the day's events and what the future would hold. Still open today as a **Toby** carvery. **(Jill Guest / W. Hazlehurst)**

OLD CROWN INN (old building), Carters Lane / Lye Close Lane, Woodgate, c. 1945. Built in the early 1800s, these cottages belonged to Thomas Ingram, a nailmaker, who according to Cossey's Directory of Worcestershire in 1860 expanded and diversified the business to include an alehouse. The pub was located close to the Dudley canal and outlying nailmaking districts such as Quinton, Northfield and West Heath. As the original business slowly died out, the selling of liquor became more important! The old property was demolished c. 1976 and replaced by a modern equivalent, still open today.

COCK, 33 Jiggins Lane, Bartley Green, c. 1969. Dating from the early 1850s, it was a former Cheshire's house. Substantial amounts of its land were sold off to the Corporation over the years. Some early taverns began as farm-houses where the farmer chose to diversify and offer alcohol for sale on his premises. With so much land to dispose of, the Cock Inn might well have been a case in point. Still open today.

SALTLEY, ADDERLEY PARK, WASHWOOD HEATH, ALUM ROCK & WARD END

GATE INN, 36 High street / Washwood Heath Road, 16 February 1962. According to the plaque on the roof, this building dated from 1873, replacing an earlier inn. Listed in Pigot's Directory, 1828. It was bought by M & B in 1919. Pub now demolished due to road widening, having been subject to a compulsory purchase order by Birmingham City Council in 1989*. An Atkinson's pub nearby at 1 Alum Rock Road, the **Tilt Hammer** is now also closed (1995*).

HAVELOCK TAVERN, 28 Havelock Road, 4 May 1961. Formerly owned by Cheshire's Brewery of Smethwick. This old local is still open today.

CROSS GUNS, 321 Washwood Heath Road, c. 1964. This former Atkinson's house was replaced by a new building (1987*) that stands close to the former Birmingham Corporation bus depot.

ADDERLEY PARK INN, 168 Adderley Road / Ash Road, 23 August 1960. Another Atkinson's pub, known locally as the "3 A's", still open today. The **Olive Branch** pub, an Ansell's house, can just be seen on the right at number 182 Adderley Road.

BRITANNIA INN, 2 Landor Street / Adderley Road South, c. 1961. A former Butler's Crown Brewery pub. The architect J.B. Surman, who had taken over James & Lister Lea was responsible for adding the distinctive stone faciure as part of a refurbishment in 1936. Closed for trading 24 August 1980*. It is now the site of a steel stockholder.

COUNTRY GIRL, Bridge Road / Parkfield Road, c. 1933, with the gardens to the rear in Parkfield Road. Sold to Punch Taverns in April 1998 but closed in 2002*.

WARD END, Burney Lane & Alum Rock Road c. 1960. The pub opened on 16 September 1927. The architect was S. N. Cooke. Pub still open today.

BROOKHILL, 480/2/4 Alum Rock Road / Brook Hill Road, 25 February 1965. The pub opened on 20 January 1928. The architect was G. B. Cox who designed the pub in Jacobean style. It was one of M & B's finest "new wave" pubs in its day (along with its near neighbour, the **Pelham Arms** that had opened in 1916) with its spacious interior and well laid out gardens. Original building is still open today, unlike the **Pelham Arms,** which was rebuilt in 1989.

The newly laid gardens of the **BROOKHILL**, 1929.

BROMFORD, 338 Bromford Lane / Farnhurst Road, 31 January 1962. The pub opened on 3 November 1927; the architects were James & Lister Lea. Pub is still open today.

SELLY OAK, SELLY PARK & WEOLEY CASTLE

GUN BARRELS, 367/369 Bristol Road / Edgbaston Park Road, c. 1969 (W). This 18th century inn was popular with stagecoach drivers on their way into Birmingham. Closed on 24 September 1978* to be replaced by the current larger building, which now is also a **Toby** restaurant. Painted a distinctive shade of yellow, it is today part of the Six Continents *Scream* chain.

BROOK, Bristol Road, c. 1961. Opened 16 May 1961, replacing an old beerhouse at 536 Bristol Road, the **Bournbrook Tavern** (also known locally as "the Steps"). Pub still open.

STATION INN, 676 Bristol Road / Heeley Road, c. 1969. The nearby railway station opened in 1876. Pub still open, having now been renamed **Bristol Pear,** another *Scream* pub.

DOG & PARTRIDGE, 748 Bristol Road, c. 1969. Bought by M & B from an independent beer retailer, 21 March 1938 and got its full licence 11 years later. Closed in 1997* and now demolished.

OAK INN, 821 Bristol Road / Harborne Lane, c. 1950. One of Selly Oak's oldest inns, which stood near the famous old oak tree until it was felled in 1906. Closed due to a compulsory purchase order, 14 July 1983*, this pub was demolished for road widening and to make way for the Sainsbury's supermarket. A new pub called the **Great Oak** opened 19 September 1985*, but didn't last for long as the pub's licence was surrendered 25 March 1994. Sainsbury's bought the land for £1million and flattened it for a forty-space car park in 1995*.

WHITE HORSE INN, 29 Chapel Lane, c. 1969. This old beerhouse was granted a full licence in 1957 from the **Rose & Crown**, 135 Bromsgrove Street. The pub stood alone for years until it closed on 4 July 1983* for demolition to make way for the Battery Retail Park

SELLY PARK HOTEL, 592 Pershore Road, c. 1925. Formerly a Holder's house. Later became the **Selly Park Tavern**. The building dates from 1901 according to the plaque above the door and featured a skittle alley at the rear. M & B also owned the building occupied by Rocks, next door.

RAVEN, Weoley Castle Road / Castle Road, c. 1946. Pub opened 20 November 1936 by architects Scott & Clark who had also been responsible for the **Weoley Castle** at Somerford Road (opened 16 November 1934). The Raven is still flying high today.

SHELDON & GARRETT'S GREEN

CHESTNUT TREE, Sheldon Heath Road / Garrett's Green Lane. The 1½ acre plot of land had been purchased back in 1935 but the first building called the **Chestnuts** didn't open until 19 July 1951 at 208 Sheldon Heath Road, receiving a licence from the appropriately named **Acorn**, Hill Street. Its nickname was "Cobblers". The current building was opened on 16 November 1964 featuring the *Rowan bar* and the *Willows lounge*. Garrett's Green (now East Birmingham) College can be seen next door. Pub still open albeit with minor alterations.

Two views of the interior of the **Chestnut Tree**, 1964, showing both the bar and lounge respectively. The lounge was renamed the Green Room in 2002 in honour of the ex-landlady.

CHESTNUT TREE, bar

CHESTNUT TREE, lounge

CABIN, 392 Sheldon Heath Road, c. 1960, which featured Uncle Tom's, *Room* and *Kentucky Room* with a wooden panelled effect. The pub opened on 21 July 1960* replacing a temporary premises which had been trading since 6 September 1951. In turn, a new pub, the **Mazeppa**, later renamed **Radley Arms** that opened 1986*, replaced the Cabin.

THREE HORSESHOES, 2102 Coventry Road / Horse Shoes Lane, c.1948. Formerly under Bass administration, it was leased to Berni Inns in the 1960s. This building by architect Wood & Kendrick replaced an earlier inn, which has now itself been replaced by a new one on the same site, c. 1982.

STIRRUP CUP, 208 Horrell Road / Bray's Road, 28 August 1956. A temporary premises was first erected on this site, before the pub opened on 26 April 1956 receiving a licence from the **Mitre**, 64 Ledsam Street, Ladywood. The architect was A. Edwards. Still open for trading.

DOVE COTE, Cockshut Hill, 25 February 1965 which featured The *Loft* bar and The *Fantail* lounge as well as the outdoor. Note the M & B's wine and spirit merchants *House of Liggins* delivery van on the car park (far left). The pub opened on 21 November 1963 receiving a licence from the **Vesper Bell**, 1 Blythe Street, Ladywood. Still trading today.

ARDEN OAK, Arden Oak Road / Coventry Road, c. 1965 which featured the *Arden Oak Room* and *Greenwood Lounge* around the corner as well as the outdoor. The pub was opened on 18 November 1965 receiving a licence from the **Australian Arms**, 232 Highgate Road, Sparkbrook. After extensive rebuilding it is now a **Harvester** restaurant.

SMALL HEATH

COACH & HORSES, 325 Coventry Road, opposite junction with Green Lane, 1 April 1961. Sandwiched between Cobee Textiles and Shelly's Chemist, the courtyard can be seen at the rear of this beerhouse, which gained a full licence in 1955. Closed for trading by 1981*, this whole block has now been demolished.

BRIGHTON ARMS, 356 Coventry Road, 1 April 1961 (W). This building replaced an earlier beer and wine house, opening 5 March 1929. The architect was H.W. Hobbiss. Between the upper and lower windows, note the M & B logo engraved in stone. The car showroom at no. 354 was Small Heath Motors. Pub still open.

GEORGE & DRAGON, 692 Coventry Road / Mansel Road, 5 January 1965, featuring the Falstaff Bar and Hotspur Lounge. Pub opened 21 September 1961 on the site of Mansel Motors with a licence transferred from another **George & Dragon**, 134 Steelhouse Lane. Pub still open today.

right
BLACK HORSE, 61 & 63 Green Lane / Green Lane Terrace, c. 1963 (W). A well signposted pub with doors leading to the *Bar, Outdoor, Smoke Room* and finally: *Smoke Room, Club Room and Garden*! This beerhouse gained a full licence in 1949. Still open today minus some of the doors.

below
NEW INN, 55 Muntz Street / Swanage Road, c. 1925 (W). An old beerhouse that gained a full licence in 1955. The price list in the bar window lists M & B Export Ale and Extra Stout at 5½d (2p) per half-pint bottle. Pub still trading, now called the **Nest,** its former nickname.

above
FREEHOLDERS ARMS, 58 Hawkes Street, 25 February 1965 (W). Another beerhouse which gained a full licence in 1955. Pub closed 31 March 1974* for demolition and a school was built on this part of the street.

left
SYDENHAM HOTEL, 155 Golden Hillock Road / Anderton Road, 25 February 1965 (W) by which time this was a Bass hotel and pub. A boxing club used to meet here in the 1920s. In 1992* it was replaced by new buildings - now a large **Munster Inns** hotel and **Delaney's bar** occupy this site.

WELLINGTON, 118 Muntz Street / Dawson Street, c. 1960. A beerhouse that gained a full licence in 1957 from **Copes Wine Lodge**, 120 Great Hampton Street. Pub closed 31 March 1974* for demolition and a school and community centre have been built in this area.

NELSON, 153 Grange Road / Baker Street, 18 April 1961 (W). Mentioned in Pigot's Directory of 1828. This former Atkinson's beerhouse is seen here in bright sunshine. Closed in 1977* and is now the site of a children's playground.

Outdoor, 21 Muntz Street / Wright Street, c. 1963 when Kathleen Angela Hudson was the licensee. Bagshaw printers and Maurice's shoe repairers are at no. 19 & 17 respectively.

SPARKBROOK & SPARKHILL

BLACK HORSE, 118 Stratford Road / Kyotts Lake Road, 2 April 1961 (W). This building dates from 1880, replacing an earlier inn. Listed in Pigot's Directory in 1819; for many years it was an Atkinson's house. One of the more unusual activities that took place in the grounds was the meeting of a Racing Pigeon club. At the newsagents next door (a house owned by M & B) the headline in the Sunday Express reads *The Day When a Submarine Surrendered.* Both the newsagent and the pub have survived today but the shop next door has now been replaced by a petrol station.

WOODMAN INN, 2 South Road / Henley St, 28 November 1979. Seen here shortly before demolition in 1980, housing now occupies this area.

TALBOT, 55 Highgate Road / Larches Street, c. 1930 (W). This beer and wine house was a new purchase by M & B in 1929 and received a full licence in 1957 from the surrendered **Welcome**, Great Lister Street. The **Talbot**'s licence was surrendered on 16 January 1977* and the pub has now gone, as has this end of Larches Street. A green is now on this site.

TURNERS ARMS, 108 Turner Street / Ladypool Road, c. 1958. This beer-house gained a full licence in 1951. Pub closed for demolition, 8 February 1976*, replaced by housing.

GEORGE, 176 Ladypool Road / Alfred Street, 1 April 1961. This former Atkinson's pub is still open and is now a Courage pub.

Outdoor, 26 Long Street / Spark Street, virtually opposite the **Warwick Arms**, 9 November 1959 when Marie Laura Wells was the licensee. This outdoor looked like a small pub at first glance. Subsequently replaced by housing.

SPARKHILL

ANGEL HOTEL, 207/9 Stratford Road / Ladypool Road, Sparkhill, 8 May 1967 (W). Dating from the early 1800s, it became an Atkinson's pub from 1908. Some attractive features including a mosaic floor can still be seen here. The Clubroom wing seen at the rear in Ladypool Road was added later. Pub still open.

ANTELOPE, 512 Stratford Road / Baker Street, Sparkhill, 1924. One of M & B's flagship new pubs when opened on 17 April 1924, a new licence surrendered from the **Royal Oak**, 13 Stoke Street. The architect was H. W. Hobbiss whose name is inscribed above the Stratford Road entrance. Note the sundial on the Baker Street side, with the inscription that reads: " I tell the bright hours only". The interior is still remarkably in tact to this day. The most interesting room is the front bar featuring carving on wooden panels and pillars, a stone fireplace and brick-tiled floor. At one stage, M & B sub-leased all the row of shops from the Salvation Army building up to the pub, including the tobacconist, left.

STRATFORD STORES, **Outdoor**, 36 Stratford Street / St. John's Road, Sparkhill, 6 September 1960, when Mary Smith was the licensee of this Atkinson's off-licence. A Walls Dairy Ice Cream cone and wafer is advertised in the window at 6d (2½p). This part of Stratford Street has now been knocked down.

Interior view of the smoke room, The Antelope, 1929. Note the M & B Deer's Leap fireside mat.

STECHFORD, LEA HALL, KITT'S GREEN & TILE CROSS

BULL'S HEAD, Station Road / Flaxley Road, c. 1960. Later renamed the **Manor House**, this former Atkinson's house closed in 2000*.

NORTH STAR, 189/191 Station Road / Lyttelton Road, c. 1960. The pub opened on 29 July 1960, some thirty years after M & B had bought the freehold. Received a licence from the **Grapes**, Heneage Street. True to its theme, this view shows the *Polaris Bar* and the *Observatory* room. Not shining so brightly today, as the pub closed in 2001*.

YARDLEY ARMS, Yardley Fields Road / Rosemary Road, 1 April 1961. A former private residence. Now called the **Mill House** bar and restaurant.

RICHMOND, Richmond Road / Bordesley Green East, c. 1960. The pub opened 18 July 1930 and the architects were Harrison & Cox. Still open today boasting a remarkably original interior. This includes an assembly room (the door of which still bears the original brass plaque); a serving hatch into the lounge, which also contains decorated ceiling beams, wooden panelling, stained glass windows and a fireplace.

IRON HORSE, 356 Flaxley Road, 1966. The pub opened on 4 April 1966 and replaced a temporary premises that had been there since 1951. Its licence was granted from the **Carpenter's Arms**, Hospital Street, a pub that had closed due to bomb damage. Its nickname is the "Tin Donkey". Here we see the interior view of the lounge when new.

MEADWAY, 105 Kelynmead Road / The Lea, c. 1962. A pub had been planned on this site as far back as 1939. A temporary premises had opened on this site on 23 May 1951 with a licence from the **Dog & Partridge**, 165 Lee Bank Road. The **Meadway** opened for trading on 12 October 1962* with a full licence from the **Anchor**, 35 Benacre Street, Highgate. However even this building was demolished and replaced by a supermarket in 1992*.

LEA TAVERN, Lea Village / Hurstcroft road, 25 February 1965. This former Butler's of Wolverhampton pub was later renamed **Tavern on the Green**. Pub closed in 1994* to be replaced by housing.

WHITE HART, East Meadway / Gressel Lane, c. 1932. The locals are sitting outside admiring the splendid cars. They'd have a job to do that now, as the cars would be parked in the middle of the busy road junction with Tile Cross Road!

WHITE HART, Two views of the **White Hart** showing various buildings at the rear prior to refurbishment, 1959.

WINSON GREEN

GOLDEN EAGLE, 233 Lodge Road, c. 1964 (W). The pub, located at the side of the infamous prison, was not renewed as a licensed premises on 2 February 2001* but the building still survives, having been converted into appartments. Nearby, the **Devonshire Arms** further down the road at 178 & 179 Lodge Road / Musgrave Road is still open.

OLD MINT TAVERN, 356 Park road / Dover Street, 12 May 1965 (W). This beerhouse was granted a full licence in 1962. Closed for trading 1 February 1976*. Industrial units now occupy this site.

SOHO TAVERN, 407 Park Road, / Factory Road, 22 November 1961 (W). Pub still open

GRAPES, 116 Bacchus Road, 1 June 1960. The architects were James & Lister Lea. Houses have now replaced the pub, which closed in 1992*. Commemorated by Vineyard Close that now runs right through where the pub stood.

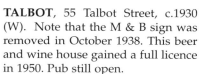

TALBOT, 55 Talbot Street, c.1930 (W). Note that the M & B sign was removed in October 1938. This beer and wine house gained a full licence in 1950. Pub still open.

QUEEN'S HEAD, 115 Aberdeen Street, c. 1962. This beerhouse replaced an earlier building in 1937 and was granted a full licence in 1950. Pub still stands today although modern dwellings have replaced the old terraced houses either side of the pub, fondly remembered by the locals. An **outdoor, 1 Aberdeen Street** was unlucky in that it had to close in 1959 due to a compulsory purchase order by the Council.

OAK TAVERN, 77 Lansdowne Street / Peel Street, c. 1956 (W). Originally it was a beerhouse. Pub closed in 1977* for demolition. Houses now occupy this site, at the side of Dudley Road (now City) hospital.

HEATH STREET TAVERN, 309 Heath Street, c. 1964 (W). One of William Butler's chain of pubs he operated before joining forces with Henry Mitchell when beer was still supplied from the **Crown** at Broad Street. Due to a compulsory purchase order, the pub closed on 10 July 1977* and passed to Birmingham City Council. Like its near neighbour the **Albion** at 187 Heath Street, it was demolished for redevelopment.

RAILWAY INN, Wellington Street / Vittoria Street, 26 July 1951. Dating from 1900 by architects Wood & Kendrick in typical terracotta style, the pub closed 15 September 1993* for eventual demolition, although at the time of writing part of an interior wall is still standing. A scrap yard now occupies this site.

Outdoor, 80 & 82 James Turner Street, 26 July 1951. This outdoor, run by Florence Mary Paice, had an old fashioned look to it even by the standards of the time.

PUB CRAWL DOWN DUDLEY ROAD

BIRMINGHAM ARMS, 38 Dudley Road / Heath Street South, c. 1962 (W). This former Atkinson's pub still survives, little changed externally to this day.

OLD WINDMILL, 84 Dudley Road, c. 1962 (W). This former Holder's beerhouse gained its full licence in 1950. The architect H.W. Hobbiss carried out alterations to the frontage in 1936. This traditional-style pub is still open.

WHEATSHEAF, 194 Dudley Road / Icknield Port Road, 1 June 1960 (W). This former Atkinson's pub is still open.

YORKSHIRE GREY, 381 Dudley Road & 1 Winson Street, c. 1962 (W). A striking example of a pub by Henry Naden who was responsible for the **Woodman** on Easy Row. Latterly part of Henry Mitchell's chain, it was earlier owned by Samuel White, landlord of the **Bellefield Inn**, a homebrew pub in Winson Street. Pub still open with a good carved back bar and old clock still intact.

LOCOMOTIVE ENGINE, 500 Dudley Road, c. 1962 (W). This pub stood next to the M & B brewery at Cape Hill and opposite the **Cape of Good Hope** pub on Birmingham's boundary with Smethwick. The Grove Service Garage, 19 Shenstone Road was amongst the pub's many let-offs. It closed for trading 6 July 1994* and was demolished to form an extension of the Cape Hill brewery car park which took place as part of the Cape 94 refurbishment.

YARDLEY, SOUTH YARDLEY & HAY MILLS

BLAKESLEY, Clements Road / Blakesley Road, c. 1960. This pub opened 17 July 1931; the architects were James & Lister Lea. Later renamed the **Village Arms** and now called the **Innisfree**.

YEW TREE INN, Church Road / Stoney Lane, 1929. Opened on 22 January 1926 as one of M & B's new wave of reformed pubs. The architects were James & Lister Lea. The pub sadly closed on 26 July 2000. In 2002, the pub's fate was sealed: it was to be demolished and replaced by shops.

HAY MILLS TAVERN, 1001 Coventry Road, 8 May 1967. A convenient local for the factory next door, Latch & Batchelor Ltd., wire rope manufacturers. The former Bass pub closed in 1983* for demolition the following year due to road widening.

REDHILL TAVERN, Coventry Road / Redhill Road, 1929. Opened on 17 September 1926; another of M & B's reformed pubs, this time by architects Harrison & Cox. Note the distinctive wooden carving which reads: *St. George, he was for England and before he killed the dragon, he drank a quart of foaming ale from out a British flagon.* Pehaps the ale in question was M & B's infamous Brew X1! Pub still open.

BULL'S HEAD, 1283 Coventry Road / Waterloo Road, on a rainy 18 April 1961. Business was good at this former Butler's hotel, judging by the number of fine looking motor cars that were parked outside. Alas the pub closed on 24 October 1983*, due to road widening. Its licence was transferred to the **Old Bill & Bull**, the former police station over the road at 1308/18 Coventry Road.

SPEEDWELL, 225 Stockfield Road / Amington Road, South Yardley, c. 1955. Opened 18 January 1929, the architects were Bateman & Bateman. Its licence was surrendered on 24 May 1991* and now a car showroom occupies this site.

JOURNEY'S END, 262 Clay Lane, South Yardley, 1 April 1961. Pub opened on 2 October 1939; the architects were F. W. B. Yorke. Pub still open today.

NEW INN. HOW TO BUILD A TEMPORARY PUB

NEW INN, (temporary premises at Gladstone Road). The old building, a former Butler's pub at 1539/41 Coventry Road, South Yardley closed on 8 March 1964. While the new pub was being built, temporary premises opened a day later at a new site on the corner of Gladstone Road. Eventually the current building opened in 1983.

The site is cleared and the foundations are laid..

The prefabricated sections are lifted into position and secured...

Alert everyone around as to what's going on...

The "cellar" is put in...

A view of the spacious interior and bar...

All finished and ready for business!

ACKNOWLEDGEMENTS

Many of the photographs used in this book were taken by Arthur Mumford in the 1940s and 1950s. His son David pays tribute to him as follows:

Arthur Mumford was trained at the well-known Birmingham photographer H.J. Whitlock & Sons. In 1927 at the age of 23, with the help of his parents, he established his own business at 243 Gooch Street from where he worked for 34 years.

He described himself as a Camera Artist. His main business was commercial, including architectural, engineering, builder's progress, litigation photography, commercial art, industrial design and catalogue layout. However he also did portrait and wedding photography; developed and printed holiday snapshots and sold cameras, roll films and other accessories in the shop.

He did his own work from start to finish. He worked from glass plate negatives; hand retouched, developed and printed, trimmed and mounted into albums as well as designing catalogue layouts all on the premises. Photographs were produced in black and white. Sepia prints were hand produced by a mixture of substances kept in brown jars and bottles marked POISON. Black and white photographs could be hand coloured to order.

He worked for many large companies, one of them being **Mitchells and Butlers**. For many years he photographed pubs both before and after refurbishment and also pubs that were due to be demolished. He was always busy, with a full order book. He was a perfectionist who was creative, paying as much attention to detail whether it was for a snapshot or large mural.

Arthur Mumford didn't just do photography, he lived and loved it and this fact revealed itself in his finished work. He was truly, a Camera Artist.

Author's note: The legacy Arthur Mumford left us is reflected clearly in the pages of this book which pays tribute to his fine work.

Arthur Mumford

To **Cape Hill & Six Continents** grateful thanks are extended to: Sandra Bright, Robert Cartwright, Wilf Donaldson, Carol Hartill, Trevor Hartland, Sandra Speers & Ron Stanton.

To the **Photographers**: David Mumford & family of Arthur Mumford; Stephen Hopkinson, John Whybrow (Birmingham) Ltd; Charles Male Industrial & Commercial Photographer, Blackheath; Reilly & Constantine, Birmingham; Leonard J. Shepherd, Birmingham; James Tustin, Bearwood; Weatheroak Press, Birmingham, Tony Usherwood of Sidney Darby & Son Ltd, Great Barr.

To **Birmingham City Council**: John Bowen; Kim James; Allan Lines; Roy Partington; Wayne Pell; Steve Spence.

To **everyone else**: John Bick; Carl Chinn; Simon Collyer; Lucy Dearn; Margaret Donnison; Stephen J. Dowling; Vincent and Yvonne Edkins; David and Karen Hassall; W. Hazelhurst; John Hicks; Tom C. Hill; Brian Lund; Kieron McMahon whose excellent website contains much interesting information: log on at www.midlandspubs.co.uk; Anthony Page; Terry Price; Anthony N. Rosser and Keith Turner. Not forgetting Gary Kilminster at the Lord Clifden, Margaret & Dennis Dovey at Prince of Wales, Cambridge Street.

To **Birmingham Central Library**, especially Peter Drake.

BIBLIOGRAPHY / FURTHER READING

ABC of Small Heath and Bordesley Green	Bob Marsden
A History of Greater Birmingham - down to 1830	Victor Skipp
A Trip Down The Flat	Gary Smith
A Walk Up The Green	Gary Smith
Aston Remembered	Victor J Price
Birmingham Buildings The Architectural Story of a Midland City	Bryan Little
Birmingham Inns and Pubs on old picture postcards	John Marks
Birmingham Pubs	Keith Turner
Birmingham Pubs 1880-1939	Alan Crawford, M. Dunn & R. Thorne
Black Country Pubs	Robin Pearson & Jean Wade
Broad Street Birmingham	Norman Bartlam
Hall Green and hereabout	John Morris Jones
Handsworth Remembered	Victor J Price
Harborne Remembered	Victor J Price
History of Birmingham Vol 3 1939-1970	Anthony Sutcliffe & Roger Smith
Ladywood Revisited	Norman Bartlam
Old Ladywood Remembered	Victor J Price
One Thousand Years of Brum	Carl Chinn
Pub Memories of Summer Lane and Newtown between the Wars	Pauline & Bernard Mannion
Public Houses and Entertainment in Digbeth and Deritend vol 9	Tracey Duffield & Joseph Black
Public Houses in Harborne	Victorian Society
Selly Oak Past and Present	G. Dowling, B Giles, C. Hayfield
The Bull Ring Revisited	Victor J Price
The Great Stone Inn, Northfield, Birmingham	Stephen Price & Nicholas Molyneux
The Quinton and Round About (Vols 1 & 2)	Anthony B. Rosser

Directories

Kelly's Directory of Birmingham, various years

Pigot & Co's National Commercial Directory for Warwickshire, 1828

Pigot's Directory of Birmingham, 1829

Sketchley's Directory, 1767

White's Birmingham Trade Directory, 1869

Reprints of most of the pubs featured in this book are available. For further details, please email **info@maxamcards.co.uk**

STOP PRESS... ONE MORE FOR THE ROAD!

VESPER BELL, 1 Blythe Street / Ledsam Street, Ladywood, 19 November 1957 (W). A highly unusual name for a pub, from the Greek poet Hesperus, named after Venus, the evening star. Seen here when still an Atkinson's house, it closed a year before the takeover by M & B. Demolition had already started in earnest and at the time of this photograph, the pub was the only building left standing on the north side of the street. Blythe Street had been renamed from Chester Street in 1887 no longer exists today although Rann Close follows part of the course of the old street. This lower part of Ledsam Street has also now gone, and the site of the pub which closed on 29 December 1958* is now contained within the grounds of St. John's Primary School. Its licence went into suspense until a new pub called the **Dove cote** was opened in 1963 (see page 117).

WHAT CHEER INN, 71 Alston Street / Johnstone Street, Ladywood, 2 December 1958. This block dated from 1857, according to the stone plaque. The houses either side of this beerhouse were formerly owned by M & B and had passed to the Council in 1952. By the time of this photograph, the Johnstone street houses had been bricked up, although H & F Parkes bookmakers' shop can be seen at no. 73 Alston Street. The What Cheer was the only example in Birmingham of this unusual but friendly name. Note the name of the pub engraved into the glass. The pub closed on 27 December 1959 thanks to a compulsory purchase order by Birmingham Corporation as the relentless demolition of Ladywood's streets gathered pace. Johnstone Street, which connected Monument Road to St. Vincent Street, has now gone, as has the northern part of Alston Street. This area is now covered by part of Guild Close.

WHITE HOUSE, 99 Unett Street / New John Street West, Newtown, 20 November 1957 (W). Unett Street was named after Colonel Thomas Unett, a hero from the Crimean war. Dominating this junction for many years, this distinctive building escaped demolition in 1958 and is still open today as a Holden's pub, although all the other buildings in this picture have now gone.

DOLPHIN, 174 Irving Street, opposite Sutton Street, Lee Bank, 1954. In White's Directory in 1869 this address is listed as a whip thong manufacturer - the mind boggles! The surrounding houses date from 1835 but no. 174 was later rebuilt as a pub by James & Lister Lea and became one of Henry Mitchell's pubs. Featured a club room on the first floor and a sign by the door indicated that the Edgbaston branch of the British Legion met there every Friday at 8 p.m. The posters (right) are advertising Goldberg & Johnson, labour candidates for the 13 May 1954 municipal election. This pub closed 16 October 1960 subject to a compulsory purchase order as part of the Bath Row Reconstruction Area. Housing now occupies this site and a school's sports field was built over the top end of Irving Street.

SUN INN, 217 & 219 Bristol Street / Sun Street, 1954, (W). On the threshold of the city centre, this building was previously listed as a hotel. It was another in Henry Mitchell's chain of pubs. An interesting looking building that looks as if an extension was built onto the front of the Bristol Street side. M & B also leased the Sun Garage next door and Robert Morris, Seed Merchants at no. 221 until these buildings passed to the council. The pub closed for trading 31 January 1965 due to the road widening of Bristol Street which involved knocking down the whole of the west side of the street. Other pubs along this section included the **Bell, Victoria, Nottingham Arms** and the **Red Cow**, Horse Fair; all of which were lost around this time. Sun Street, which ran from Bristol Street to Spring Street, has now disappeared under the Lee Bank Middleway.

BELL, 57 & 59 Bristol Street / Great Colmore Street & Bell Barn Road, 1954. A former Butler's of Wolverhampton pub by architects James & Lister Lea, dating from 1886/7. The distinctive ground floor semi-circular arches in stone were a foretaste of a successful style they later adopted in other pub buildings. Note the bell set into the wall above the entrance to the lounge as well as the fine glasswork denoting Bell Vaults. Next door stood Bocker & Bettridge's Dance School and Dennis's House Furnishers. The pub closed on 10 June 1965, another compulsory purchase order due to the widening of Bristol Street.